A ROUG

C000098052

For Many, Ven & Les —
bedtime stories for
all ages.
love
Helie
17/3/2002

By E. A. Markham

POETRY

Human Rites
Lambchops in Papua New Guinea
Living in Disguise
Towards the End of a Century
Letter from Ulster & The Hugo Poems
Misapprehensions

FICTION

Something Unusual
Ten Stories
Marking Time
Taking the Drawing-Room through Customs
(*selected stories*)

TRAVEL

A Papua New Guinea Sojourn: More Pleasures of Exile

EDITOR

Merely a Matter of Colour
(*ed. with Arnold Kingston*)

Hugo Versus Montserrat
(*ed. with Howard A. Fergus*)

Hinterland
Caribbean Poetry from the West Indies & Britain

The Penguin Book of Caribbean Short Stories

E. A. Markham
A Rough Climate

ANVIL PRESS POETRY

Published in 2002
by Anvil Press Poetry Ltd
Neptune House 70 Royal Hill London SE10 8RF
www.anvilpresspoetry.com

Copyright © E. A. Markham 2002

ISBN 0 85646 337 X

This book is published
with financial assistance from
The Arts Council of England

A catalogue record for this book
is available from the British Library

The moral rights of the author have been asserted in
accordance with the Copyright, Designs and Patents Act 1988

Designed and set in Monotype Bulmer by Anvil
Printed and bound in England
by Cromwell Press, Trowbridge, Wiltshire

ACKNOWLEDGEMENTS

Versions of some of these poems have appeared in the following
magazines, journals, and newspapers: *Agenda*; *Ambit*; *Calabash*;
The Caribbean Writer; *The Coffee House*; *Kyk-over-all*; *Poetry
London Newsletter*; *P.N. Review*; *Poetry Review*; *Proof*; *The
Rialto*; *The Sunday Gleaner*; *Trinidad & Tobago Review* and
Wasafiri. 'All Our Oases' and 'For the Environment' appeared in
the anthologies *Montserrat Versus Volcano* (1996) and *All Are
Involved: The Art of Martin Carter* (2000). 'Taking the Drawing-
Room through Customs' first appeared in *Voices of the Crossing*
(Serpent's Tail, 2000).

Contents

POSTSCRIPT

The Long Road to Barnes & Noble, Booksellers   11

PART ONE: *Poems 2000*

Photocopying Your Story   17
The Man With the Umbrella   18
O, The Humiliations of this Life   19
Psalm 151   21
Black Youth   22
Inquest   23
It Gets Worse, My Friend   24

PART TWO: *From Montserrat*

To Whom It May Concern   29
Hurricane, Volcano, Mass Flight   31
Two Men at the Cassava Mill   32
Lines Composed to Test the Idea of Montserrat   34
All Our Oases   38
Nearing Sixty   40
The Last Letter to a Grandmother   43
Allies   47
Re-entering the Caves of Castine   48

PART THREE: *Late (from the last century) News*

On George Lamming's Couch   53
From a Waitress at the Franziskaner Hotel,
    Wurzburg, 1999   54
Insomnia   56
Night   57
My Brothers and Sister are Alive   58

Hidden Extras   59
A Philpot and a Wife   60
Peace Process   61
The Paraffin Stove Case   63
The Husbands   64
Whistling in the Dark   66
A Life   67
Double Act   68
Vulgar Assumptions   69
Interruptions   70
Friday the 13th   71

PART FOUR: *Remembering*

On the Death of George MacBeth (1932–1992)   75
Pierrot   77
On Hearing of the Death of François Mitterrand   78
For the Environment   80
Remembering Geoffrey Adkins   82
Appropriator, Hijacker, Racist, Thief . . .   84
Hidiot (a polemic)   85
Old Man Horace, Oowokalee   87

PART FIVE: *Taking Note*

Taking the Drawing-Room through Customs   91
In Other Words   105

All Relative

C.B. Fry was once invited
to become the King of Albania.
He graciously declined.
Yet, that's far easier for the mind
to accept than a capped and whited
Zog opening against Australia.

DAVID SHEILDS

'I encourage them, and they encourage me;
and that's what life is all about.'

TONY BENN, *talking about a visit to the House of
Commons by a group of pensioners from his then
Chesterfield constituency*

Postscript

The Long Road to Barnes & Noble, Booksellers

I

I copy this in a fair hand
no longer like a prescription for those who know
the code, or a diary of someone cheating on a partner;
and try again to arrange the lines in BEFORE &
AFTER an event the world knows about.

BEFORE is to be forensic agent of your luggage;
so much paper soiled in scribble, markings
open to interpretation: they will sniff these symbols.
Is disquisition on the thoughts of the SECOND MURDERER
in *Richard III* to go unchallenged through US Customs?
(A uniform, a gun, a dog.) So, in the spirit of self-censorship
change SECOND MURDERER to *SM* and hope to raise
a prurient eyebrow. That, and much more under BEFORE.

And yes, far away the poor eat less than we do.
Near home someone is blaming his mother for all this.
Over here, the theater opposite advertises *Hedda Gabler*.
So, if aims still fail to fit their outcomes, outrage
and relief not quite in sync, no one knowing what is changed,
I play my part balancing feet in each worn argument
and stay trapped uptown, a voyeur far from carnage;
and avoid, in penance, visit to a favourite bookstore.

At small ceremonies of friendliness and bafflement where
    we eat
the servers pour water enough to slake a desert, ice left
in each glass like a guilty tip.

AFTER, in an affordable hotel the television brings us Sunday
    morning
pictures of how the world looks. A man with preacherly roll
of fat at the back of his neck giggers about the stage, microphone
in hand, his jacket screaming. The sermon might be
that whatever happens in the world, the comic
is black: his "Oh oh oh ya ya ya ya ya ya" parody
of grief, "The Lord is with me, the Lord is with me
A gatta get outa here, A gatta get outa here", won't drown
the terrorist's simple text: "The time for fun and waste is over."

In time Peshawar drops into your line of poetry
bringing your reference up to date. Statistics of the Arab world
cascade like free offers in the supermarket, and make you wary.
Not apocalyptic text, not the supposed gulf where gulfs matter
but something surer to provoke vertigo. Average age in Pakistan
and Saudi: 19 years – Second Year students at university.
Jordan and Syria are still in the First Year. The Yemeni at 15
is at school. Though the Maghreb – there's a word – and Egypt
can, at 22+, be invited out to dinner without fear of arrest, where are
the bourgeoisiefying middle ages? You get my meaning
from someone in lived-in Britain, average age, 38.

III

And so I head for the Village and get lost in tacky
Asia, new Americans selling trinkets, huddled
between landmarks not yet theirs: the Bookstore
is a man across the street selling newspapers.

But there it is, green and old-gold liveried as if proudly
bowing you in. Upper floors rustbrick and tasteful
as if sheltering the family: will children of off-Broadway
hawkers find it? The upstairs café for browsing
helps reshape this trip. Here, with a bowl of soup
you flick through the e.e. cummings someone left you
and relive meeting-places of long ago, Penny Universities
       where a Dryden
came in person, Addison rhymed with Steele, and the Astors
       and the Vanderbilts
(Oh, my patient house-slaves, I'll tell your story, too) – Astors
and Vanderbilts who lived here, conjured the shades
of Dr. Johnson and Hogarth and Davey Garrick over dinner.

And yes, weeks on, something proud of its disfigurement
Lower Manhattan smells of burning dust and metal, Third
       World
chic – like the other half, living a life. At night, near
where we lodge, a man, dressed like a commissionaire
sings and dances in the doorway. Again, a man looking
like Donald Rumsfeld sings
and dances in a doorway. High above the street,
like a Health Warning, *Hedda Gabler* is on offer.

Part One

Poems 2000

Photocopying Your Story

In a library long ago you absolved me
of the *detail* of librarianship, poor cousin
from the big house of authorship. I knew then who you were.
But failure of talent, of luck is punishable still
by a rule-book, somewhere. And your story, undelivered,
long merged with others nearer home
looks like being lost. So, does it matter?

You and you and you from grandmother
to friend to wife have crossed the frontiers
in my luggage, much revised: why won't you make sense
in that language, in this climate? For no new version of you
squares with a shared memory and the force
of one man's claim to intimacy.

And here we are growing desperate. Though prepared
for it, some of us have died, catching me unprepared:
this is not a book, I can't just write in deaths
without blame, even here where no one knows our secrets;
and this must not subside into a parody of loss,
and this must not be passed off as lament.

So here we are on a weekend in this place
that houses thousands. Lights on in as many rooms
as I can manage, countering the drizzle and the quiet.
In the basement a machine that promises to extract
poison from the air collates your story. From outside –
wish you were here – the radio brings us bombings, shootings
over territory. You're safer with me here, unread.

The Man With the Umbrella

Not wanting to point the finger, I credit him
with suffering one of those small mishaps
which seem, at his age, hard to put a name to,

like trying to figure out how time had slid
by in the traffic; and whether it was too late now
to do something about it. Or should he be grateful

that no huge shock to the system had stopped him
in his tracks. Though maybe this was a man
less haunted by my own obsessions. I see him, then,

as coming back from the dentist, anaesthetic
beginning to wear off, so the umbrella is a sort of public
shield to balance the new gap. I look around

for other umbrellas in sympathy with this ploy.
And the one that comes into view is neatly folded:
To give him support, like a fellow sufferer

shames me slightly. 'It's stopped raining,' I say,
holding out my hand to the elements. And his smile
is not unkind. And now I am wondering if I'm wet.

Oh, the Humiliations of this Life

Heard the one about the plumber
And the floozy where no one laughed
At the end for though plumber

Was a woman of grace and delicacy
Like wife, like daughter and mother
Of your dreams, making the case

For floozy as male rapacious scum
Seemed to be pushing the PC thing too far.
So, let's start again, folks.

The book, oh Lord, has been written,
Written and read; writer and reader confused
And tired. You are your own

Opponent now, trying to outwit
A meaner self: here I am on the canvass,
Here I am arms raised, scorning

Your cheers. So why am I doing this,
Doing this past its season? To send
A message, old love, to you

Never good at reading the signs,
Puzzled even now, by this stale play
Of I say special, you say pleading:

And there were, indeed, angels dancing at the Ritz.
And when you turned and smiled at me
A nightingale sang in Berkeley Square.

And yes, we agree to disagree such messages
Should be simple, like a dedication
On your book where nothing furrows

(Forgive the language) the brow;
And your name is spelt the same from book
To book, a gift of manners;

Ah, but we move on, we make mistakes.
Yes, this is one form that courage takes.
And your name spelt from book to book

Hints now at cleverness, of something
Cloudy and strange, like a change
In climate of a country we have known.

Psalm 151

Blessed are those who die before birth
Removing temptation from child-killers and abusers.
Blessed are the dumb, blind and insensate
So that the abundance of this world
Won't drive them to frenzy, madness and despair:
Blessed be the Lord of such things. (For, lo, the music
Of the times is yet made by the enemy.)
Blessed, too, the ends rather than the beginnings
Relieving poor creatures of the comedy of hope: that way,
The Wise Ones say, leads to disappointment,
Which is the room prepared for you without a partner.
Blessed, then, is the God of stone
Who ignores the teasing of the leaves on call them trees,
The gratuitous green of grass, the mirage of water,
Silking along the ground, like an old temptation.

For those of us who have tasted, seen and lusted
After these things, and have lost them
And are exiled from the hope of return to that feast
Must seek out a greater God of Mutilation
Where each world serves as well as the other,
And one day is a century is too short to measure,
And eternal death is on offer without prejudice,
And Circumference and Stone and America are one.

Black Youth

D'you think it's easy for your mother,
he says, like a bully, to have so many black people
around the place; and he the blackest person in our house.

And last time when my sister was naughty,
he threatened us with Big Destructions
and Punishments Too Terrible To Name.

And he's not supposed to threaten us
even when my sister hits him in the face
because she's still violent at that age; and biting

her arm and counting her fingers wrong
when she's got all ten, is bound to make her mad.
And it's not fair when we complain

because my mother only smiles or sighs
and says he lets us call him bully because he spoils us; and yes,
it's hard having one *really* black person in our house.

Inquest

So he opens the door to the Mews, too sober for the porter
in *Macbeth*. Before that I ring up to save face: this is beyond
the call of duty, etc. You deserve a bit of respite
at the weekend. Sorry . . . Kind of you. Just in to use
the computer. And printer. So both buildings,
I'm afraid. Any time. Half an hour would be fine.

So he opens the door to the Mews, and the pun
on the word he's heard before, so a new thought squeaks
its way in: which one is he, exactly? This keeper of keys
is a man with a name. To stop him thinking the obvious
I offer the joke about both of us having a home
to escape from this early on a Saturday.

So he opens the door to the Mews thinking me
an impostor. I suspect this figure from Security, dressed
for all seasons, might blunder into what I might write today:
he's at home with music and a book, and photogenic
wife and daughter – upgrading the Hockney portrait
of Bradford seen from California.

So he opens the door to the Mews and I think
how he must vote. Never too late for dialogue
to show we're professional at this game. So I pull
an old trick to ease us through this; and apologize
in advance for the *Brief Life* not written: he'll understand
about the laptop at home letting me down, etc.

So he opens the door to the Mews like a different man.
Where's your friend today, I say it, prickling
as eyes slide away from call it intimacy:
*the uniformed man in Ibiza with a student? Go for it, then;
there'll be worse embarrassments on the lunch-time News.*
Actually, the porter's message is one of suicide.

It Gets Worse, My Friend

In the supermarket you lose heart
and buy something fairly wholesome
in compensation: you might yet die
of natural cause. No need, then, to dwell
on an old story told with such drama elsewhere.
And yet the drip drip of benign water
wears at foundations you thought might last.
Droplets collect and mate like early life, unnoticed,
till the end is a squiggle is a river a flood
endangering your settlement. Ah, but here I am
conjuring oceans to rinse one dark mood away.
Why is it so difficult to be casual, to bring things down
to grumbling size, like chatting with colleagues at lunch
about the photocopier. Till these, too, relapse
into PC recruits for the enemy. One, who shares my subject,
targets me for disquisitions on cricket. Another,
spurning, as we do, the queue to compromise
mouths his solidarity, like a remedial
listener, while I speak. All this, I know,
seems less urgent than the story of the wrong-
looking man shot from a car belching along a Leeds
or Leipzig street. Or of your friend's arm, wrapped
as from war-collateral in a nurseless zone near to home.

And now a small cloud over a supermarket
promises rain I'm ill-dressed for. This is my neighbourhood,
those who serve here nod in recognition. At the cheese &
meat counter we queue in our mind careful of fair-play.
The stranger, confused, will be put right. 'I'm not sure,'
I say to her, trying to hint at an old arrangement,
'how they do it here.' And then someone, in secure
possession, comes to our aid, spraying cold water

on my years of teaching children in this city
how to renounce cliché. Her smile is understanding
and long-generationed. 'I think they line up,' she slips
so lightly out of idiom, 'behind the one in front.'

Part Two
From Montserrat

To Whom It May Concern

Like the painter-brother I didn't know
who trapped somewhere in the corner of the canvas
near-forgotten details like a particular flower in the vase
on the round table – that hint of fruit subtly true –
bringing back idle days in the flower-garden
next to the water-trough (and the mango-tree)
separating front from back yards; or –
for those who weren't there and must rely
on close readings – the vase next to the lamp
whose shade, still clouded on one side, showing,
with the jagged, burnt edge of wick, the drawing-room
not yet restored from last-night's living, and Sarah late
for her duties. So we can pause to witness the scene, frozen
in confidence, not tidied with intent
as in the more famous ones on show,
where the quality of light striking the bookcase
in a way you don't remember; or the figure of the cat
curled on grandfather's rocking-chair, edge
of the piano showing, make this house *generic*.
Why debate the obvious that we never owned a cat,
and the dog, Carlo, not allowed in the house,
would be strange substitute by people so fastidious.
But we know the argument for this licence;
that we let go of privilege of family-heritage,
and for *them*, our hosts, a statement about pets and house
countering hints of *otherness*.

So – the story goes – if hurricane and volcano and the
     carelessness
of migration have destroyed evidence of a life
before this life, one picture with its random detail
would be as good as another and work, like Lascaux,
to decave the dwellers for present company. Lacking the wrists
of my painterly brother, and the votive role

of early years; and giving up the struggle
to maintain a dialogue, like an earthling talking to Ancestors
who might be forever dead, I go for broke
and have some fun and scare the natives on the fields of sleep,
and come out brandishing a late-life secret:
I am your son, the killer, I say, *who carves your name*
on a tree in the park daring the Old Bill
to track me back to the shrine: here,
I tore the flesh of this scumbag who tore the flesh
of something in his trust. Like the surgeon you would have me,
I amputated arms and legs of two or three
neanderthals saving from frenzy of limbs the soft parts
of Joan and Karen, let's call them. Now the little stumps of Lord
& Master must perform their pantomime for a tougher audience,
good at withholding drugs. Yes, our contract runs
to those sons of Presidential bitches who have looted Africa.
Your eyes glaze over, good that you have no eyes
to recognize me or where I live, or even those of us writ large
as a warning – a boxer here, a comedian there, a sister running
round and round a track to encouragement and applause.
If these are not your children, despite the names and features
we'll get you newer ones. The world has come in for audition.

Hurricane, Volcano, Mass Flight

The five eggs in the dining-room
Must be turned each day to keep them fresh.
Their dish, still unchipped
Draws the eye of visitors. If the hens

Lay today, add washed eggs
To the prize and remove the first laid
For breakfast. Remember to dust all
Glassware and wipe the surface of the cabinet.

If there's no one left for housework
Leave one of the children behind to see
To things: the horse won't live forever
And pigs and goats are things of the past.

But fruit in the garden must be picked,
Picked up; rabbits out of the hutch
Kept down; the lawn cut, yard swept.
This house of your mother's can't be protected

By priest or jumbie or de Lawrence.
So do what you can inside and out.
Someone who grew here sniffing new bread
From the kitchen or bat-droppings in the attic

(Puzzled at the great drawing-room library
Shrunk to this size, casting the world
For family out there with a memory;
Or a neighbour alive and interested)

Will guard from afar a dining-room,
Still with its layered, breakable vase, egg-
Crowned, white on blue on white which
Like the piano upstairs, has travelled far.

Two Men at the Cassava Mill

It's here in the front yard near the water-trough,
well clear of the grass where Nellie spreads
her sheets, starched white with *blu*, to dry;
two men, one in short pants, working in tandem
grinding cassava enough to kill the village.

It's a *coffin*: the woman looking down from the verandah
at ground cassava shrouding its box, under the mill,
will not give in to the fear prickling her
to leave this place *soon* with her son, still in short pants:
she shuts her eyes not to see the men in action:

Left foot on a board, on the ground, stable.
Right foot peddling, pressing down on the pole,
easing up on the pole, boy hugging man
up and down in tune with the man who feeds peeled cassava
into the throat of the wheel. He is expert

and won't soil cassava-snow piling up underneath
with gratings from his fingers.
The man has no thoughts, he is dumb.
This is the 1950s, no one will know what he thinks.
The mother will shut her eyes at this ritual of men

intimate in public. The best she can do
is freeze the boy permanently behind
this rough man from the village: *why do they work
so well together*? The boy will change from short pants,
label the suitcases, and head for England with a grudge:

he will always be second-carpenter in this scene.
No one will recognize the force of his stubbornness
Grinding the cassava grinding the cassava
behind this dumb man in protecting the village
from disaster. For the mother is reduced

to panic, and the man in front is trapped
in *folk* memory where no *sign* translates him into language,
and anything you like *You're the woman of my dreams woman
of my dreams*
Rampant and foul-mouthed, endless in America, etc.
can be put into his mouth.

I'm writing this on a computer in England,
a boy grown out of suits, years past burying
the mother. And the man grinding the cassava
is of course dead, the village new-poisoned by ash. A volcano,
this time. And who wants, anyway, to grind cassava at a mill!

I'm writing this on a computer in England
remote from the house, no mango at the back, no grape-
vine facing the edge of Mrs Meade's land: this
could have happened anywhere; the cassava smell has gone,
and nothing colours the evening air with home

but a vast night that prevents you sleeping.
And I sense what the dumb man might have thought,
and console myself. And I indulge the image of a mother
protecting
her son. Yes yes, you say: but what's this got to do
with the price of coffee in Brazil. Or murder in Kosovo?

Lines Composed to Test the Idea of Montserrat

'It's like the month of May in Andalusia'

> Christopher Columbus's *Journal*, the Italian sailor on 'discovering'
> Guanahani (San Salvador) and later Dominica (1492–3)

I

Your voices change in exile, who's to know
how you will read this line: I'll bury it
in a book for safer keeping.

The young girl on the cover, appley
and wilful; and the man from Andalusia ready
to bite into her, seems about right:
though we don't know yet he's the man from Andalusia
the point is made. I'm writing an autobiography,
was born there, grew up here, etc.
Somewhere I'll lay claim to heritage, why not Irish;
so, to get there I won't start from here, sort of thing.
Here, you see, is the wrong place. Today the US George
Washington, no longer a man on horseback but a ship
(minus slaves) steams towards the Gulf. Today –
a girl, her throat cut by a man roaming round England
unpunished – can't be the way to start.
So let me recross the seas like a sailor with his Journal
which my mother Francesca and Giovanni, my brother
would call a fake. Like the son of a tailor
I've discovered islands where Calibans
and Prosperos cling to the edge waiting
for the world to go round. Here, sea, sun, early-
squawking cockerels seem not to have enemies. OK:
my name, which hasn't changed much, is Pewter Stapleton.
Something by my sister Avril, the child botanist –
one of the *Intuitives*, don't you know – updates the cover.

So I'll give up on an architecture of my life
vast and cathedraled and accept its journeying through
    continents,
though sometimes above the ground, at a level
where others live. From Columbus to refugee
will your book impress friends, family low on expectation?
The house is gone, and the island; generations of ghosts
lodged here and there treat us less gently now
when they visit, unannounced, day or night.

                    II

This is a half-way house in someone's country
crowded with problems: it will shelter
one of your twelve rooms, the house cannot be got through
customs; the idea of house, transplanted in its own space
is difficult for friends even, to accommodate.
The house, rest easy, is spread over four continents
the better to preserve it. In DC, capital
of the Americas friends gather in your kitchen (736 items
reclaimed – 510 in the main bathroom) – in your kitchen
and talk of old times. In a southern
country where the language is a tease they sit
on your terrace and pour red wine and pledge your health.
Here, where I saw my first black cab, first stage-
policeman, discovered new pleasures in a tremendously
deep bath – here in an English city
I locate the library where generations of preachers
and teachers, and others near myth – poloniusy grandmothers
trading dos and don'ts – can come to browse.
All this I write in preparation for what I write.
Now for the chapter beyond exile:
Our friend in DC, his house landscaped with success
attracts veterans returning to their India. He discovers
next-door, garden fenced from garden, a house

and makes purchase, careful not to trap *his* Montserrat
under one roof: May you live to biblical age, Sir;
may your teeth outlast many dentists.
Over here, a voyage away, at a point between home and work
I claim a patch. This is where, unprovoked,
thoughts skid into old thought enough to make a pattern:
the raggedness of last night cartoons into new shape.
Low skies of the day before suddenly hint of blue.
This is a healing space larger than home or work
in a drizzly northern town: this patch of spirit
in the body's random trail is one traveller's bounty.
A friend, who is clever, promises to transfer it intact.

III

All doom and gloom; not a bit of it: no May Day signals here,
no new rituals for the burial of the dead,
no speeches rehearsed to a Truth and Reconciliation Commission,
(Our hands are stained but not with hangings, lynchings, genocide;
and some of us live, mysteriously, in Luton
which is, they claim, easier to say than Andalusia.)
I've been converted to the faith of thank-you letters. So many
soft gestures from strangers who forget
or puzzle over when you weigh in with acknowledgement.
My room for gratitude, like the famous cup, runneth over
spilling into neighbouring country like an offence.
Far off a mountain erupts scarring people
into thought as if at the beginning or end of a play:
One man in his workshop invents a wheel which isn't round,
to save us. Another – can he swim? – sets out to visit
the hundred and ninety two countries of the world, looking
for a seat at the UN and language that will make him
equal to the US, Palestine and Australia.
These and others – a woman called Molly whose business
is private – will crowd our fictions. And me? Ah –
Comme ci, comme ça. Ça va. Em Nau. Alles ist Klar, alles is klar
And *Was ist los in Luton?*

*

I read somewhere that people tend to die at four
in the morning. Well now, I'll tell you how I saved
some friends. I tempted those at risk to sleep in daylight
and rise for breakfast after 3 a.m. By four, the eating one
is saved. This science earns me credit of red nose
and floppy shoes like others reconstructing the island
from Flood, Fire, Hurricane and Volcano.

The fiction is pre-history, a stressless time and space
free to unbuckle into a life without meaning,
when someone in the garden saw an apple fall and made nothing
of it; and no one has memory of reading Wordsworth
on the verandah. The present is a chapter rich
with private jokes and riddles of being young and free
and reading Proust and grilling sardines in old Portugal.
Till one reader smiles into intimacy. Like something
from the botanist unpressed and green-veined once again:
this flush of kindness restores our faith in magic.
She's leaf-scented, rustling a static Sunday into life.
She is, indeed, our entry into light. This is –
She is the month before the month of May in Andalusia.

All Our Oases

Grandmother declined to walk
or wear her teeth except on Sundays
when visitors, ignorant of new sounds
in the family came to lunch
to be verandahed with tales of pioneers
from this house making it abroad:
she had no need to show she could walk.
Much later a midnight film reminded us
of unfinished business: there, an old man
wheelchaired, wearing out wives
and relatives muscling him out of cars and lifts,
their threat and resignation played for laughs,
grew bored, got up, strode off. Suspicion
that childhood magic lost
in our meandering years might work this time,
conjures back the faithful.

First, there's the Open Letter signed
Horace, mad and marooned on the island
building his road between family camps;
this helps us to travel back in time
when we were sick on the ferry, terrified
of toy aircraft meant for others. Horace, holy fool
was First Admiral recharting Signor
Colon. Through him we promised grandmother
naval victories the history books ignored;
we promised her to marry and be good
to wives and children of cousins less lucky;
we promised to make her walk.

And how to update an old letter
while folk at home cling to their mountain
sniffing sulphur? They send scouts
to claim new space. (Will this chunk

of Zaire, that misnamed American state
be enough?) The island erupts, erupts
with something like anger, impatient
of old farts abroad nostalgic for their childhood season.

And here's a brother from the north of England;
he has seen Australia on a Sheffield
pavement – dry patch in a sea of wet
every inch Australia: you knew those islands, faces, trees
that form in clouds real as aeroplanes?
Only, this pavement Australia held shape
till passengers got aboard; he has been there
often, learnt the lingo. Now change in climate
denies him Australia, he signs up for our road –
along with artists re-imagining scenes tourist'd
by hurricane and volcano. Let's pretend
no time has passed, grandmother's undead
and Horace, Ancestor-like, Very Reverend
of his own church, choirs hope across water
with those tales we used to tell ourselves.

Nearing Sixty

for Eudora Fergus

Two weeks here and time to depart. The 5 a.m.
cockerels, lurid as painting
at the start of the holiday, now stitch patterns
of sound round auditioning dogs and crickets
as if to stress some theme in this quilt of remembrance:
if they knew of your complaint, the hostess seems to say,
they'd mute this third world welcome. The illness, though,
sounds like a boast to prompt a chorus.

Nearing sixty: I imagine it in letters,
less threatening than numerals whose lack of flourish
and courtesy – like something harsh, not softly
counting – prod you to revisit stretches
of life underlived. O, for Walcott's one-sentence poem
at nearing forty, managing, in the end without bitterness
or pity, to rhyme sleep with weep. There will be a party
when the time comes. I am packed now, again,
for England, looking neither forward, as in '56,
nor backward through a life skirting comedy –
though the jokes, the jokes have gone missing!
England, then, for the *festschrift*, friends rounded up,
their forced cheerfulness making you stutter,
brave, greying heads, somehow lyric and dignified
as if saved from a wreckage. Here are the pioneers
who discovered no new land to rename
after decades of travelling. Drink, then, to the attempt,
to near-misses, and check that something which you might call
the ship's log is written up in our script.

I'm thinking sixty can't be where you disembark
with Accountants from England and German bankers
whose native thrift balloon into magic pacifics
grass skirting young bodies, or in mind-swept tuscanies

beyond Provence where my poolside prejudice
twenty-five years ago rejected, in short lines
and in narratives more indulgent such late, life-weary
resting places. For I, too, may have planted a brick
here or there and watched it grow, like unearned income, into
    villa,
casual as the thought of travelling to Australia.
(A mistake, then, to have travelled to Australia.)
I can see us standing here, drink in hand, children
of friends itching to know when duty is, in duty, done.

So it must be here, back here, the island of origin.
A Sixty in good shape, to be remembered as simply fading
and distant, not gaga and twisted into some joke-recycling life-
form due to residence abroad. Not even like uncle George
back home in the '50s, Panama and Cuba and Haiti
turning him bitter. Islands cannot sleep
in case they vanish in the night: watchdogs
will worry any bone seasoned abroad till the neighbours
flesh it new; and the story of our travels will stand
retelling. From Boston to Stockholm; PNG and the Forbidden
City, you bring relief from familiar Canada and Britain;
though the Brother who soldiered in Africa upstages you still.
Once, like a new comic, you did the rounds
seeking audience outside the rum shop or with yard Characters
under a tree, folksy, as in a Selvon story. Now home is a test:
hurricanes and volcanoes have checked our progress, exxing
out certainties: this friend, well-housed in another's home
    laments
life in the shelters. This stains the talk. Gone is the League Table
of advantage for those who left the island, so we prick
the bubble of our ambition – and did you hear
the one about the girl in the supermarket, her hat at an angle?
Ah, it was worth travelling the world to see that hat!
Your stories of Cervical Spondylosis from 40 years of manual
typing (or from Railway portering) maintain the post-modern
    note.

Two weeks here and discovery, magical as Columbus.
I am calling by accident on someone of a past age.
And here she is, a girl in a dress bleached
like washday making you nostalgic, as it should.
Her face, uncreased, will be our calendar, absence
of teeth not spoiling the line. A beauty preserved.
She tells the story too perfect for a book.
Propositioned seventy years ago, she almost blushes,
by my father, she has survived the generation intact.
(She might have said yes, said yes too late.)
A found mother: no disloyalty to a mother who in winning out
must have suffered from her triumph; Wish you were here, too.
Two mothers; what luck, as if to renew my apprenticeship
as son – and this time it will be better, better.
She is like a flower ashed in the garden between Eden
and after-life. I balance flattery and apology;
(What precision of speech! 'I'm not too lonely, I listen
to the voices from the radio and the television') and recall
a dream of my sister, skipping, young, and of my grandmother
materializing as a baby yet to talk: This makes me cautious.
For my eyes are open; and this mother lives alone;
and – another thing – you can't assume that friends, scattered
on four continents, will assemble for a birthday.

The Last Letter to a Grandmother

(From Athens, with a partner; from London, without)

Not like a friend's whose last letters to a wife
litter the floor or the beach now, like wrapping,
as he probes the horizon for sign that she will come back
pre-suicide: this poetry of atonement is not for us.
Time to be naked: I have lost touch with, ah, grandchildren,
a grandmother in the way, errands for a house not lived in
these forty years, and behind that the house where ancestors
    grew
into spirits, the source of narrative. This is a monument
built outside a plot of history, decontaminated
by a freed people's obeah. I was clever, I was
the simpleton who took words at their value. In the beginning
was grandmother's grandmother, eighteen thirty-something,
    so much
accomplished by one birth. And the next generation, women-
    and-men
carved into awe, like Greeks before Christ, the colour
of family: Uncle Ned, a Doctor, his brother a lawyer
and the JP (which one was he? who came, twice, to England)
    all preserved
from the elements, unlike blood and muscle, in our private
    museum.
Even your teenage sibling joined the Parthenon when
on a Sunday she played the organ in the Methodist chapel.
    Follow that,
you dared me early and often. Follow that through the
    confusions
of England. But England was 40 years ago, a lost life.

So Athens: I look back now at the wreck of more modest hopes
for the family, swop with dawdlers at the foot of *this* monument,
modern pygmies unalarmed at their own size: no one strives
to explain the statue's missing head and arm,

or to convince us how the winged creature once flew.
So I will treat you with detachment of these Greeks chomping
through salad and souvlaki knowing that Athena –
goddess of war, goddess of fertility – and Pericles, and the other
    fellow,
whatsisname – all these alliterative grandmothers, survive their
    mountain.

And now for life in the present tense.
The present, like a revolving door that slips us inside
the foyer of a foreign hotel and out again on a familiar street,
affords relief, like day-time television,
till something you took for granted shudders and stalls,
first like an ill-kept engine, then like nerve and flesh
ouch-ing accusation at neglect of what's at hand.
These moment to moment moments challenge loyalty to the house.
Thirty years ago I watched a friend kill his father;
at the end of the play Actor led his Actress to a rented room.
I alone scoffed; I knew too well that plays were tricks
you bowed out from when the night's work was done.
(And was not killing the father premature
when father, though not lost, had to be tethered to family
before the ritual with the knife? He went by natural cause, *Oh
    Father
Which art in Toronto* . . . side-stepping us as always). So foolish
to prolong this affair with the past, like writing
letters to a grandmother gone to dust.

II

In case you rely on it, grandmother (you're not a patient
in hospital, or in a home on the edge of conscience), in case
you're finer now than dust, more like a cloud
and take your shape through memory, let me blow something
from the past towards where you might materialize.
I honour a contract to bring you up to date. Imagine
me, then, partnered here in Athens. Imagine Athens

and partner, new provinces to our kingdom giving home
a hinterland always promised – though our talk, uncreolized,
would not be permitted in the drawing-room at home:
this talk in Athens is beyond our range of tolerance.
We changed rooms twice today, once for privacy
then for a balcony in the sun (wrong side of Acropolis) where
    a partner
might smoke: Love . . . *O, Love, O Careless Love.* How did
    bachelor
uncles in this family conquer the world?
Theatre of Dionysos. The Odeon of Pericles. Treasures
galore. And why are boys from the island unable to pleasure
their women? Unanswerable questions scuttle you
back to comfort: clutching at (remember?) baking
at weekends, and auctions in the animal pound
and church on Sunday. For now, oh grandmother, it's war with
    the elements.
The island, whose name you never knew, is less than it was.
We are refugees now, and most of us know it. My card says:
This is Athens. Wish you were here. The house,
though not the land, has long gone. We are the talk of the town
because our mountain, dome-shaped, now a saddle, leaks
fire and anger and chokes in white dust the rider in his
    helicopter,
the supplicant on her knees. This splatters our pride
as a settled people. What trick of family will survive it? It's late;
I've let you, again, steal another day from us. There's a woman
on the balcony sobbing into ash; and, yes, we are accused.

    III

And I explained it all away as if it were fiction.
And so I'm in another part of the country, call it
England: King's Cross (and what does the cross mean, and who
is the king?); and does the time of day allow
for a happy ending? I'm a guest
in a house damp and cabbagey, a stage-set

where a man kills a woman and hides
bits of her in the river: someone on the television
tells us how it's done, knowing the furniture here
will not slide around the room in bafflement;
and in the morning there will be breakfast with strangers.
I hide all night in a deep house as from
a hurricane. On the roof, astonishing in their beauty,
filling the sky, are mammoths, not horses, male and female, who
    must be eased
down without demolishing the house.
One false move and the beautiful objects
slide into nightmare of flesh rebelling its age –
a drip in the arm, a limb amputated, foetal granny
enduring the four-letter world of pain. In the morning –
Ah, in the morning, calm, the house intact, mammoths
in another part of town, you take an old partner
to a favourite place for breakfast, and count your luck.
For this is a game of endless chances. This is
family that lives forever – though some, like cheats,
die young. Here is another part of family, someone
on the balcony wishing to enter. In this version of the story,
there's space for her, and for her gods which will topple mine.
But you've failed to meet her where she is (a little voice says)
and the search is on (O, endless, endless game) for something lost.

Athens/Montserrat, June–July 1997

Allies

He picks a path from the old house to the village
as if to buy fresh bread at Mr Lee's,
because the flour has run out, or weevils
make grandmother think twice about risking it;
and the floor of Mr Lee's shop is well-swept,
and his habits thought to be clean.

This is not a joke exactly, an understanding, maybe,
between someone out there, call him Horace,
and one over here who answers to Pewter
content to talk across water. If the house can't be found
and Mr Lee a memory smudged by the elements
and slow evacuation of the village

Pewter would have to grow random about Horace,
a cousin now with an interest in the house,
or a contemporary remembering the way things were,
or anyone curious about these myths.
But Horace saves him from the dignity of fiction,
as he walks back along the path to the village.

Re-entering the Caves of Castine

The hurricane exposed what initiates
and the unknowing claimed as the Caves
of Castine, the lost 'church' of St.
Caesare, pre-Columbian, magical. For some,
the Caves were the scene of Immorality
Acts and, like the dormant volcano, a threat
to society better not harped on. Nadine,
down from Barbados, hopes to explore them
for her thesis. She interviews us
a couple of generations late and is unlucky.
She knows about Amerindian myth and precautionary
baths in the zinc tub with herbs
that helped us into adulthood, helped
to protect family abroad and counter
the obeah of neighbours who prised parents apart
and made children fail their exams. We are
our grandparents who spoke in hushed voices,
reserved for Africa, for Haiti,
of these matters. Nadine asks questions
of men they'd prefer to answer after dark,
all too sly to know of initiation rites
of middle-class women before the journey
to England and imprisonment
in the houses of their sons. And the priests
of Castine who serviced them so well they lived
half a life of exile, without sex: how is this
possible? Nadine is led from well-swept
ground to the gaudy carpet displaying
a story of the Caves more to our taste;
this, the great binge, the Jump Up street party
provoked once a year for tourists:
three days' licence for the wife to live
off-island with her lover and no badmouthing
commentary; the mistress free to flaunt herself

in the family drawing-room and the Castine
of the day to throw off his garb of priest
and (with conniving Caesars) play Antonio
to the barren Calpurnias at hand.

Bored with Europe the world comes to witness
us at play, a new Oogodagou: TV cameras
take us home to warm the winter; magic, songs,
the unaccompanied dance of renewal. And then
talking in tongues and (oh yes) sacrifice
to show how far we've travelled.
All this is documented to death, but middle-
class women of the '50s visiting Castine
to stock up for a lifetime without sex abroad
leave no clues in these Caves, tongueless after
hurricane, and mocking Nadine's thirst.

Part Three
Late
(from the last century)
News

On George Lamming's Couch

So, she comes down in a nightie revealing
more than she intended: something has disturbed
the Sunday-morning snooze: *what are you doing here?*
She asks the stranger on the couch. She has seen him
in the street, one of his colour: does he speak
her language through those lips? Can they spirit
themselves through the keyhole: *what are you doing here?*
Though the house won't be paid for, it seems, in this lifetime
she holds the key to the door: what hill did he climb
to breach these walls; there are no weapons on him
that she can see, and his body in repose reminds her
they are said to be cunning. *So much black skin
on her couch: is it hot to the touch?* That's right, two men
in the house, before breakfast. Last time the government
promised an end to rationing: will every home now have one
of these for Christmas? Luck of the draw, maybe;
she has been warned what happens to a girl
with a will of her own: did peeing on the rubble with her friend
lead to this? His eyes seem to see her crouching
on the site, and here she is naked in a nightie. He's up
on two feet, reading her thoughts. He speaks through a mouth
of uncovered sex. And she will stand her ground
checking he's left nothing on the couch. *I live here.*
His voice close enough to trip her over: the curtains
are his; does he know curtains from nightie? She won't
call for help till she's ready and dressing-gowned. Standards:
I'm English and this is my castle. She will banish
fear and do the normal thing; ask for evidence
of his claim to the couch. You get away with things
when your nerve holds: will he touch her before
she can wake the house? And through those lips, yes, he asks
to go to the bathroom. So he can't live here, after all.

From a Waitress at the Franziskaner Hotel, Wurzburg, 1999

We are grown into tolerance, my friends
Support grannies and trees in places
We might never visit. No jokes now
About deck-chairs on early-morning beaches
Of my father's time: we take our turn like the rest of them.

And when he came into the restaurant I didn't flinch,
Just reflex tightening of thighs and creepy-
Crawlys up the back to your neck. Yes,
I saw him on television that time (those times)
And how did he get here so far from Rwanda?

And the decades of preparation against instinct
Will prove us changed. The table is white:
I and my blouse are white. There's a lily in a vase on the table:
He will be dazzled with white. He will think of brides
And brides and brides. He will worship Germany.

And then, then he claims to know –
With a million dead in his own country –
That one wine is dryer than another wine. Good.
This is good. Then his grilled fish comes
And he insults the judgement of the Chef

Who is not a Gastarbeiter. I have studied Latin
At the Gymnasium, yes, and toyed with voting
For Herr Schroder. My friend has been to the Turkish
Cafe in the north. Though we can't screw around because
Of Aids and black babies, we are not my father.

But Turk, Ostlander, Slav and black man
Who escape bodies in their village come here
To sip white wine and monitor our taste. This one
Instructs us how to grill the fish. In the hotel his bed
Is made the normal way. And will there be complaints in the
    morning?

And will my father always be right?

Insomnia

Guilty of ambition, that's right, leaving the culture
behind: where have you earned
the long view? Others find their measure –
the bushman overarching weapons before the fight,
the new boy eyeing the school bully –
and survive. It's late in the day for you
straining towards hinterland and empire.

You are, admit it, afraid of dreams
that reduce you to something in the bathroom
mirror. Upstairs, armchair doctors want to strip you
for the couch marked Childhood
with Atlas and tracing-paper, fitting continents
of privilege to geography which stays in place.

Now you're in company with those who live within their space.
This one, a stranger, stands less straight because
of an accident or a surgeon, and has stories
to chime with yours. It pays to be attentive and gloss
misfortune so no one comes out a loser with family
from hell, or on a street grown foreign with gunfire.

Where are we now? This new map you're tracing
(baggage falling away into an ocean of sentiment, a splash
of sex) leaves you spent on a rock
defying vertigo: no need to shout for a neighbour
to complicate the story. Tomorrow, you will reorganize
the diary of comings and goings; now, with an eye open
while someone sleeps, you plead insomnia.

Night

Teach me, nevertheless, not to be consumed
by regret: that voice on the phone
fractured from family, wish it good health,
long life and better music than I allowed
in support. I wake from screech and flare
of traffic of another man's success and, hearing you,
forget the bafflement – left stranded
wrong side of the road – of that random woman's
preference of partner for something more obscure
than human. Stop me, then, bullying
a small talent to confine itself beneath us,
to feet, well-hidden, the colour of clay.

One luxury of talking to yourself in a world
of people is hope that no one might hear
till you get it right. Unrehearsed I say: I'm not good, true
or able to prevent, on this November night,
nineteen ninety five times late in life,
one fist surprising the promise of a face;
and in the morning somewhere a child
will be startled into adulthood. There's no one around
to mug us into logic.

And who weighs time and finds it heavy?
And who says it's mine now to carry?
(To mourn one friend and bury another
might be my detail.) Though in separate houses we watch
the evening news and envy those after *Guernica*
still young with disquiet. The voice which brings this on
fades, yes, by agreement, like the house-manager
bringing up the lights on a private play.
Outside, it's Sunday morning in a provincial
town, a day to be reclaimed for one missed early –
no telltale papers – and in the evening, dinner with friends?

My Brothers and Sister Are Alive

I'm writing this in a square in Italy
Instead of the postcards I won't now send.
The new address-book presented no hurdle
To brothers and sister still claiming a place
Under the alphabet. Though a dozen others didn't make it
To the clean page: what sort of scribe are you to lose
Those names? At times I think of recompense
Appropriate to the newly dead, and shift the frame of guilt
To hear them speak. (Ah, but let the state, the church,
The professional malcontent who would scorn my caution
Deal with the – call it history.)

Family, distracted elsewhere, assume me safe.
I must respect that and not exploit sense in this time
Of need. Still suspicious of drawing attention
To our luck – like those plants that don't flower
And provoke little interest: can this be enough
To save us? A public gesture on my part to signal
Surprise and gratitude, unlike the gifts we exchange,
Might seem showy, an act of wilfulness
Breaking a spell. So keep your council, tourist, admire
The Cathedral, observe the strong legs of Italian
Women crossing the square; and write the postcards.

Hidden Extras

She washes up, hush, before they are up.
Cutlery, crockery, oh dear – a servant
would rethink the status of family
from knives, plates come to this: she's needed, then,
to protect the house. Pots and pans
to be wiped and put away. Ah, so that's it!
Where have they hidden the kitchen towels?
It couldn't be a visitor, unwelcome, in the night
with silver long gone from the trunk, wedding-
ring broken by a man who wasn't her jeweller
lost in the crossing: would it be burgling with contempt
to walk off with tea towels stained and holed
to spread rumours of people living like migrants?
She spends who knows how long tugging
at a thought. And there it is; no need
to panic, towels wrapping bread, snug
in their carrier-bag. So breakfast won't be stale
despite everything. Pots and pans, wiped,
belong in the cupboard; she can regain
her room out of sight, unhaunted, like the sleepers
who will recognize her when they discover the morning.

A Philpot and a Wife

There is no other identification on his body.
Not dead, they taunt the wife who isn't his.
She comes to hospital to pronounce him alien
to class and race: that portrait is not of family.

Her husband, the doctor, wears no uniform,
has never thrown her down the stairs (wrong house)
nor, in the shower, helped anyone to slip on soap:
she must stay sane, despite the change in life.

Another deep breath, the children are off her hands
to conjure daemons. So to her challenge
from the wrong side of town, a Philpot without family,
the size of guilt; protector. There may be worse to come.

She sees him pummelled, a presence in the garden,
a '60s throwback, a Pinter matchseller. Could it be
her lover stuck for words? But women here are spoken for.
At best someone will use Philpot to shore the losing

argument. So give him four lines to say his piece.
Stripped of nonsense he can't fill them, but mumbles
something about a daughter who has problems with her kidneys,
and of Herr Doktor, uniformed, wifed, who caused it.

Peace Process

Yes, negotiations started on board ship
(oh, pre-*Tiger*, pre-*Fearless*) somewhere
off the Canaries when, with nothing left
to be sick, Philpot vowed to complete the journey
and repopulate mothercountry with issue
the colour to raise him from indignity
at home. He would come to port
at London's Manor House or Paddington,
or sail north to Leeds and sire a team
rising in grim times to defeat England
at Headingley. If that was the pact,
and Pewter a boy-mascot on board allowed his book
as calling card to a house closed to others, a primer
to gain him audience of (who knows?) macmillans
and gaitskells, his equals in class and intellect –
boy & man together could outflank the enemy
before the start of hostilities.

So would they agree, old man and older man now,
on terms of the reunion? Philpot
back like the past with wounds to show for it,
a neglected accent, speech without nuance,
still no reparation for things ceded in his name
no interest in the bank, etc. to draw on –
and all those claims he didn't need to spell out –
turns up, of course, like an old plan.
So now: how has the scholar filled the time?

Pewter's welcome is fluent and soothing
as if it were rehearsed: it's clear this voice
has glided through contracts, won accommodation
and concessions enough for a peace process;

we trust it for it knows secrets kept secret
from us: better not to enquire after safe houses.
So we go with the rumour that someone is sheltering
a Philpot on the run, and no-good children
are roaming the streets looking for action.

The Paraffin Stove Case

*Your survival, remember, is in not letting them know
who you are*; so we answered to the wrong names, etc.
But that's not where I want to start the story . . .
        It was years before I threw out your old stove; the family
grew attached to things, making light of the danger.
You might think of me as the lodger or neighbour,
other side of the wall no longer offering protection
when lovesounds switched, like a bachelor's radio,
to something difficult to wank to. So that was my condition,
Your Honour, dazed and unthinking when I rushed
to throw the danger out. Burns and bruises, let's call them,
to the family having healed, I cite in defence.

And, of course, in life, you must accept some penalty
for coming to the aid of a neighbour in distress;
though my frenzy, say those who console me, was compensation
for decades of not acting when the cry was on my side
of the wall. I make them up, friends who seem concerned
that I'm denied the sight of spring, a pint at the local and – oh,
less bearable – raw bumps of promise gendering your dresses.
Now, you can ignore me and get back to the family
in question. No need to read this next confession,
for who knows if time has passed, and your temper changed:
here am I confined in a flat, the house unguarded, the street
looking maybe like yours . . . *That's not where I want to end
        the story.*

The Husbands

Tonight, he will talk of the rivers
Of the world, quoting old Mitterrand; and I
Will counter with churches, Cathedrals, mosques. This jabbing

At torso with a fist of speech triggers commentary
By partners off-stage, tired of blood-sports. They
Have already thrown in the towel:
What's to be learnt from this but who controls

The vocabulary when the story is next told?
We agree, don't we, that partners are the travel-companions
We love best, when they adopt us as strangers humouring

Our foibles. (The day she was Cleopatra, kind to her bargeman.
And then Liz to his Richard gigoling down the Rhine.
Me too: she was with me last year in Umbria

(No shortage of placenames to frolic) at the Temple
Of SANTA MARIA DELLA CONSOLAZIONE:
I blasphemed her Pope's right boot proffered
To be kissed to a dazzle of silver, which is her due.)

Ah, the acts of omission that divide us. So we fault
The map of countries not discovered, and hint at dialogue
With the cartographer who thinks we're too old to travel.

And the talk amongst ourselves meanders past river
And Tabernacle to remembered scenes of the children
On holiday playing near a pool and painting the world crayon.

That's cool, you know, like who ate well in Vilnius, Lithuania
Or in Shanghai before the burgers moved in. And did you
        know
That the Ristorante Mino on the Via Magenta in Roma
Is the worst hole in the universe? Ah,

By morning, bless you, our friends all fit the vocabulary
Of blame; images of dough rising like sex, yeast
Us through the night, new bread for partners
Who think they know all about breakfast.

Whistling in the Dark

Some good will come of it, you say,
shaking off the lake like a dog. Later
on television a glimpse of someone

haunts in a way less personal than that holiday.
You saw her see her have seen her
in the street, in a cell, in a country ripe for reference.
In your notes, though not in dream you deprive

yourself, like the athlete dining with friends,
of some trifle – all put on hold over years that glory
tempted you. And now

alone at that hour when unfinished business
seems again your business, you seek her out for apology
and make another note; your prescription for tonight.

A Life

Today I adjust
the favourite wall
of a lover.

The vine it supports
won't arbour us
as promised.

The old arrangement
looks odd to others,
to us;

looks like another
country
we must have known.

Double Act

Are they together, we ask, with *her* upstaged
as he recites the poem about commitment? And look!
Her back to the audience she begins to disrobe,
welts on the flesh caught in the lights.

Between the acts we talk amongst ourselves.
Off-stage effects of beating and humiliation
drift in. Then the poet comes on with a body-
language right for stumbling through his lines.

He is finished. It is done. He stands distraught.
His talk of loving and sharing falls short
of what we expect. He apologizes for labouring
the point like an amateur. He invites questions.

Vulgar Assumptions

I discount vague threat in the air
as if suddenly vulnerable to attack:
subtle forms of harm seem to lurk
in the traffic, in the next pedestrian
erupting into frenzy; even in the trees –
branches falling naturally as you pass:
It's the title Professor that does it,
as if elevated beyond protection
of the standing army who draw no envy:
A friend – I once put him in a book – sandwiches
foreignness well against fire-bombing
or more sanctioned forms of protest
by lodging within the enemy: he will not live
in a house, detached. Silly, I say, vulgar
to assume the label makes you today
more valued than a Mister, a chained exhibit
of memory, prize specimen at the bidding.
All this I say and try to believe. And yet,
already there is a call from someone
watchful of my interest: Take care, she says.

Interruptions

This is a gun to the head, to your head
(I have not learnt to shoot but you don't know that);
in my hand a text, not translated,
of addresses and dates (memorials, too)
where family found shelter and moved on.
(These few rounds in the air make you watchful.)
Our scribes and mountebanks dishonour
the line. Now, with grey hair, in a hurry,
I must pass on a house unsafe for habitation
to children, knuckling under, growing narrow in the space.
I come to interrupt the politics, breaking off
from my books where a certain person of Xian,
or someone called Minapwan in a highland province
of New Guinea reveal something of my grandmother
who, on a small stage, played her parts well enough.
Reparation, I leave to the children trained
to speak this text authored by others. The gun
is weighty like the sex you feared to meet.
It measures a space where we walk. It's a crook
for lewd folk crouching in the hedge
(If this goes off which of us is safe?)
and if this goes off which of us is safe?

Friday the 13th

First, the bad news: Thursday the 12th. I take
the blame for missing out on some trivia, fearing
carelessness here must prologue the bigger
thing I won't name. Tomorrow's decision
will change something; it's too late to think
of Friday the 13th as an ally.
So tonight I celebrate bad news as if this were a pledge
redeemable at the end: no need then
for tricks with salt over the shoulder
or furtive knocking on wood: that pre-emptive strike
should do it. Yet, who can trust this symmetry?
I think of analogy from sport that fail to convince.
So I force myself back into weighing chances
for tomorrow: the Committee (not so comic now)
who cup hands for your escaping humour, will joke
about the date: will this help? Aren't these the straws
that stagemen reach for? I won't go on with this,
I will read a book. Phrase after phrase flickers
into portent: 'The fat woman stepped into some mud
and lost her shoe.' That's me, of course, denied a place to hide
in the past tense. In this safari haze
I am an oddity in the party, my place in the jeep
resented; so in the mud I effect this small
gesture of humiliation which one visitor photographs
and another will describe, willing me to read.
Well then, do the decent thing and go to sleep.
I will not lay in champagne like semi-finalists
at the Benson & Hedges, to sneak back, speech crumpled,
with apology to the shop. Fitful sleep, I tell myself,
where failure to remember a classic author
lost me the dream-argument, is but an eating disorder

I can live with.

It's early in the morning (I don't know yet of any *obits* we must write) and I resolve that Friday the 13th will be a day like any other. Only better. Touch wood.

Part Four
Remembering

On the Death of George MacBeth
(1932–1992)

As it comes in the middle of a private drama,
as such things should, to restore balance,
I don't wish to appropriate your death.
Your name, much dropped in lines by colleagues,

weighs anchor now: a ship of poems? Sailing where?
Let me say to the living: DO NOT WATCH
THIS SPACE but for stray evidence
that those who survive a few years longer

will do the decent thing by friends when necessary.
Of our age, like the elder brother
who scared us with his heartbeat
till he resurfaced to make US Vice Presidential

jokes possible again, your body-stutter, George,
was more serious. I'm talking to you again, soon
no doubt to boast friendship (safer than this
stab at *intimacy* bound to baffle

as with the inattentive partner, uxorious
in public): you will not contradict me.
Let me claim brotherhood and leave it at that.
This is no public letter, no large statement

to rival epitaphs of the great dead – Auden
on Yeats; Walcott on Auden. But real enough to hold
at bay coarser thoughts – that with one name cancelled
we of the stranded army shuffle sideways, close up

towards the front of the Anthology which you might
have edited. Your voice was familiar-strange
and good to hear. Your poems took risks like
all your costumes. You might have performed a little longer, man.

Pierrot (1974. Spéracèdes, France)

I'm taking your name, my friend,
away from you. You never gave permission
while you lived: thus revenge
of the living on the dead.
I'm not going to say the sun
is dimmer or even that your good-
neighbourliness made the world a better place
(but your bulk in the hammock among the oliviers surprised,
amused us). You will be missed, Pierrot;
you helped us all in little ways, gave us
credit from your life's miscellany and died
as if we owed you nothing. You won't
be replaced by a monument in the square,
though the familiar puzzle in all our minds –
left unanswered, say, when Bob went at 30,
and now again, Beatriz Allende, wastefully –
has a new shape, squat, from Provence,
with neat, dancing shoes: how can we do less
than remember that you lived well?

On Hearing of the Death of François Mitterrand
(1916–1996)

You've been a good neighbour, it's been nice knowing you,
that from someone's grandmother preparing for exile into a home:
even so FM, your assumption of France helped to nudge me
away from islandness. But you weren't set down on earth
for this. And here I am in the library getting away with a life.
Browsing, it feels right to indulge a Mitterrandist
fantasy of excess in these too-ordered stacks.
The man's death saves me from growing into too-small spaces
where the literary shopkeepers add up, add up. I have books
in the library, a rung on ambition I daren't acknowledge: Mitterrand
personates such thumbsmudge in this place where ego,
like a magnifying glass, distorts the interest of students
taking your books out: it's timely that the great die
to divert us from trivia. I'm thinking of Nobel cocksmen
at the Elysée, and of your choosing a Russian novel
as number one 'because it has everything'. And I'll deny
counting the 63 dates stamped on my books, for who knows
if readers are honest; and to invite thought-police
into this aside is to keep me brutish still, disconnected
from the death of something grand and, nearer home,
from the dishonouring of a neighbour by her children.

Marking papers, I'm back at my desk reclaiming
something of the weekend, a stand-in God now and then
bothering to chase a thought: this student's snatch of music
tuning into argument recalls
the dial turned aimlessly on the radio where something startles
for a second before the comfort of *Start the Week* or *Woman's Hour*.
Confirmation of the death of Mitterrand prods me to response.

Why is the obvious so unsettling: need the world know
that this is personal? I'm shifted back to France in '74,
the election pluckily lost; in our Cabris house toasts of tristesse,
suspect perhaps as old hands sip pity to La France
unready for glass palaces and poetry. In our Cooperative
we built in southern stone, in brick, three years
on sites with Rene and Julian and Luigi summoning over lunch
philosophies and artists they shouldn't know
and the latest French Revolution not yet over,
to fantasize under the oliviers dancing in the street which in '81
was a little late for me. Mitterrand was more costume
to dress an ageing mirror. (I think of a man from my island
        frozen
in protest, a writer maybe of talent refusing
to devise verse and narrative till certain things righted
themselves in the world, as moi seul, contre l'humanité
would still be suspect. He didn't put landmines
and his own treatment of those dear to him into books:
he thought me quaint to cite François Mitterrand.) So now
content to take from the mirror what my face says
I return to the unmarked paper and think if grandes projets
deserve reproach, it was comme-on-dit necessary to imagine
oneself a young place before Mitterrand pyramided into glass.

For the Environment

for Andrew Salkey (1928–1995)
& Martin Carter (1927–1997)

It is cold this Christmas
I have no idea what it costs
to heat me: *God have mercy.*

The corner shop in Crouch End
selling knick-knacks
is now something else. The brothers
with children to educate

have gone back to Ireland.
Here in Sheffield two bookshops
which made us welcome, have gone
taking the space for browsing.

So we must live within our means
like aged parents
in new surroundings

(And who will respond to the old
jokes: it's the buttons, man,
the buttons rattling
in the new jacket, nothing more).

And I think of Andrew and Martin gone,
that generosity of spirit buried,
Andrew and Martin gone
their literary grandchildren

hustlers below stairs
full of frenzy, full of noise
desperate to inherit the house.

And I think of island and family gone,
and the heritage of remembering
respecting those spaces
new filled with rubbish.

And I am here, standing in
committing such things to memory
while memory lasts.

Remembering Geoffrey Adkins

What do I feel about the guitar-playing
nobleman and a Monsigneur very grand at Oxford
columned in the *obits* today? Something
middle-distanced like philosophy
in the academy: with you it's not so safe.
I hope no one overhears me talking into air
to make me check this, pass it off as a tick.
As there's no good place to start let me walk
backwards till, bumping into you, we strike
the expected note of pleasure and huddle
into sense and relief that poetry and editing
and who's up this month get slung on the hook like old overcoats
as we toast family, old family, near-family.

I remember a line in your poem, two decades ago
prickling us beyond amusement
that a man so safe could own a longing for passion
this public: we cast you in the role
of Greek Chorus, of evangelist at the rostrum
calling down some sacred text. We protested
friendship in seeing the fun of it. Those who mourn
you better knew you better. I won't compete
with family who summon you when they must,
who get stung anew with what-might-have-been:
for them loss is a deep-in-the-body wound
too mean to show dressing on the skin. So let me speak
as a friend, sporadic, as in life.

It's a Friday in March, long after the event.
I am travelling south. There will be portents
to make the day yours. Not this day every year
for friends might crash the party.
Not the whole day, even, but this bit of it,
the journey from Sheffield to London. At the Newsagents

we may serve ourselves a newspaper, unsupervised.
In London a busdriver, with the weight of courtesy,
declines the fare; and then an evening stranger
tosses 'Hello' across the pavement. All this
because you shadow me. So right, so well-proportioned.

O, why won't you let me be pompous,
recall our ambition, praise you for outliving
Shakespeare; slip into *obit* mode and see you
translating self beyond bodyweight, beyond gender –
like my mother (Say howdie to her if you see her).
Why won't you collude for a day to make me forget
my own discontents: is packing up to leave home
less than what you are? But even now your Joan,
your Jessica – and that older daughter whose name I forget –
are urging different questions on you.

You will always be 56.
I'm thinking of the O from a man who was not
Greek Chorus. Or even how I might nudge
stray thought towards something honest: if the next spread
at table hints at nothing with hooves and feathers
and shells and scales, wouldn't that be overdoing it?
I glimpse the lost island where being changed
into a basket without handles concentrates
the skill of the living. Ah, Geoffrey even now
I find it hard, like the poet, to deviate into sense.

Appropriator, Hijacker, Racist, Thief . . .

(Apology to Ken Saro-Wiwa and the Ogoni Eight)

We've gone through the thesaurus
of your names on this London bus,
conscious of echoes across the world,
and get off chastened, grown up children
falling out of step. Time still
to digress on the status of wit
of busdrivers, one brother regretting
being talked out of the car. At the house
someone's mother remembers better times
(Some of us shook hands in the street
when the country that shames us tonight
gained 'independence') when status was high;
now, as if one was a patient or creature
for handouts, sachets of salt and pepper
on the tray contain less salt and pepper
than before: we think rival things
and commend her grasp of what we neglect
(Is the murderer in uniform capable
of such detail?). Oh, Abacha, uglier
than the creatures trapped long under stone
in the cottage we renovated, we wish you
passage on the bus whose driver's thrust
draws no blood; we do not spit back
in your face, Sir, but wish you Life
and sense to know all your names
for ever and ever. Amen, says someone's mother.
And now, let us remember your victims.

Hidiot (a polemic)

(with apologies to Linton Kwesi Johnson
– and for Sani Abacha)

And now there's that other man in uniform
A bit like you fellows in uniform surrounded
(Like they fraid jumbie!) by all those men in uniform.
But, folks, we not suppose to be telling joke.
Days gone when I could come in here and say
That what we and the boys discussing is the cricket
Or whether to boycott the Australian *COON*AWARRA
Cabernet Sauvignon and the piccaninny on the jamjar;
Or whether this or that PEACE PROCESS is process to peace
Or to make the conquest and defeat look good.
But things turn bad, you know:

They killing us now, man
They killing us because we DAN-GER-OUS
They killing us because we write play (Remember time
when they used only to burn book!)
They killing us because we say: Massa, We Want Clean Water
    Fi Drink.

And we don't have no gun
And we don't have bomb
And even the words to say stop tief what we have, they tief
    from we

So you discourage and defeated
But we have a memory of rising up again
So don't think discourage and defeat going stop we
And now I look pon I-man and say (*Even though you got on*
    bullet-
proof TV vest today) I going surprise you

So why you do um?
Is not just me a say this: *why* you do um?
(Like me hearing Miss Mabel, again, from the days in Coderington
when she did ask that man that kill woman in the village) Why you
    do um?

So stop, na?
If you is big man already with stripe pon you arm, why you so
    foolish?
You know them say when you grow hand too long for your own
    pocket
is chop they going have to chop it off: so you not fraid?
(You say the world full a hidiot giving us all a beating: *I* say they not
killing we so)
You say this is poppyshow, I say you is jackarse
– You say, I say . . . –

And we end up right where we begin, calling each other hidiot

Old Man Horace, Oowokalee

(for Cousin Markie, d.1999)

In a book on the shelf a loyalty of poets
has turned your namesake into English. Horace,
we served you less well: even now I can't release
the dead man, my cousin, from a name that wasn't yours.
Too smug, of course, to ask forgiveness from no one, from
    nothing.

I will say to friends who anticipate this: I called him Horace
to protect us both; he was mad, a name-change
hinted at the shell of a plan from which the soft game escaped
to embarrass family grown less playful by the decade.
At school in Plymouth we bullied fear some thought genetic
outdoors into ambition: he won that round. In France, in
    Germany
we wrestled natives in a sport still desperate. So tell me:
were your prized daughters real? Or must Anna-Livia
and Plurabelle remain our fantasy from the curious Irish
    joke-book?

Books were to be written, remember? And so friends die
to help us bring forth poems: what better point of death, I say,
to them who censure me for not using actor's
body-language to smother such thoughts? Why this
than something sunny for last week's birth
of a child to a child? Loss of life (Yes, Sir, we are powerless)
leads us to ponder things taken for granted, to make apology
for nothing specific, and vow to be kinder today than yesterday.
    All that.

Pre-Horace years ago, in Ladbroke Grove we mapped careers
as Elvis, as Bertrand Russell, as this or that batsman on the
    visiting

West Indies team. We talked of books and promised to make good
insults to our clan: Man Friday set to swim
a sea of language pollutes us still. You *did* answer back, quick
off the block, pulling rank as Old Man Oowokalee, messenger
to Benamuckee, Friday's god of the mountain
here to instruct arrogant Crusoe of our customs, our fastidious
eating-habits. Ah Horace, when near home, in a northern town
    I walk past *graffito*
FIRST CHURCH OF CHRIST, SCIENTIST, I think of you.
(Already, I'm forgetting if you had a sense of humour.)

Old Man, so you came over the years, to embarrass us,
not just madness in the family – we're tough now – but as a metaphor
of failure in our '50s narrative where you and I, too,
are pioneers. So we abandon you, tastefully as we can
(You survive in my fiction, such is life) for no big crime, just madness
and sponging in a style that would not disgrace a proud one
down on luck. I forget who claimed most often that high ground
said by the careless, to be moral. Even now you make me straddle
certainty – the generosity of madness. Thank you, Horace.
You're not here today, but it's not a good day: the world
is frightening outside as inside the institution. And here you are
provoking a poem. Next time, cousin
I promise to fake the courage and call you by your name.

Part Five
Taking Note

Taking the Drawing-Room through Customs

I'M HANGING ON to the old notebooks despite the chance to get rid of them; for the past year a university has been collecting my 'archival material'. So I feel that all these jottings of the past forty years properly belong in a corner of that institution's cellar. But I haven't finished with the stuff, the notes and stray entries waiting to be written up. I've just packed another box of – what? – work-in-progress, discarded versions and so on. It's the fallout from my latest collection of short stories, *Taking the Drawing-Room through Customs*. And even this box I'm unwilling to let go because the stories distilled from this raw material are only part of what I mean by 'taking the drawing-room through customs'.

I see this particular drawing-room, one I've been trying to make visible ever since we abandoned it in Montserrat in 1956 for England. Though there was no particular trauma in leaving it behind – we were quite looking forward to England – there was, on coming to England, some dismay to find the general assumption was that you had left nothing of value behind. Even fellow West Indians seemed to collude with this attitude. And trying to explain yourself was risky, for this was the context – student gatherings, nursing friends of my sister's, weekend dances and cricket matches – where people from overseas were seriously, if unconvincingly, engaged in rewriting their histories: so many young Africans claiming to be sons of chiefs didn't carry conviction.

In 1956, aged 16, I managed to avoid school for a couple of years, working in the rag trade, making ladies' belts and handbags and shoes in small workshops and factories in Baker Street, Great Portland Street and elsewhere in the West End of London. I was writing at the time and trying to teach myself languages. My eldest brother, Joe, used to take correspondence courses, and my other brother, having had a year at university in Puerto Rico prior to coming here via Canada, was brushing up on his Latin at night school; so one lived in an environment of self-improvement. I mugged up on my Latin and Italian vocabulary while I put press studs in the belts and listened to *Workers' Playtime* on the radio,

Ken Dodd and Gladys Morgan doing the jokes. Bad at languages, I assaulted the foreign vocabulary each afternoon when, with a bag full of freshly made belts, I set out to do the drop for my opposite number, Ivanov. But seriously . . .

Though I wrote a novel, mercifully lost, in the late 1950s, these were the heady days of theatre: *Look Back in Anger* (1956), Beckett, Ionesco & Co. Those of us trying to write dreamed of fulfilment on the stages of the Royal Court or at the Aldwych with Ken Tynan and Harold Hobson singing our praises in the *Observer* and the *Sunday Times*.

My playwriting debut was more modest. The first play produced was at university in 1964. That was at Lampeter, where I was reading Philosophy and English. *The Masterpiece* was, in fact, a bit of a Platonic game, idealism coming up against the reality of the body. I'd had another play in rehearsal at BBC Radio in Cardiff, but that didn't materialize. In lieu of that, the putative director, Frank Davies, suggested that I apply for one of the BBC trainee producerships. But this seemed to someone of my arrogance a diversion from the real business of writing and I declined. Very much later I realized that some of my contemporaries, better briefed – Melvyn Bragg, David Frost, Alan Bennett – had taken up offers of BBC producerships. Towards the end of the sixties, I had the great good fortune to work with the theatre critic, John Elsom, both in writing and mounting group plays in the enormous front room of his house in Shepherd's Bush. My rejection slips from theatre managements over the past forty years are enough to paper one complete wall of my study. You learn certain lessons from this, apart from the obvious: if the plays aren't going to be produced, the material, at least, might be recycled. And, indeed, my first poems were speeches lifted from dud plays and delivered at poetry readings.

It must have been about 1971, when I'd started publishing poems and stories in magazines, that I was forced to confront what I was about as a writer. The confidence – and humiliation – of publication helps to concentrate the mind, as, indeed, did the business of performing the work in public. Avatar was a poetry-reading venue in Kensington, behind Gloucester Road, which I gravitated to once a month. It was presided over by an ancient titled Lady, and you were likely to run into famous names, Sir John Waller being the most unlikely. Its abiding interest for me was that Avatar was my first meeting with the young American writer, Diana Hallett. Diana and I were soon to set up house in Shepherd's Bush and our fortunes were inextricable for the next decade.

At this time I lived in John Elsom's house in Shepherd's Bush, which was as near as you could get to being in an Arts Laboratory of music, theatre and writing. What also helped to motivate me was my experience, fresh from a year in the Eastern Caribbean, directing the Caribbean Theatre Workshop. The four plays from that period are among those still to be revised. I had misjudged my audience in the Caribbean: in St. Vincent I came over as someone privileged, from England. It was only the luck of sleeping, for six weeks, in a haunted hotel in downtown Kingstown and not going mad when the jumbie appeared that gained me the necessary credibility. In Trinidad I was held to be someone from England, but too radical to be let loose on a Port of Spain public in the wake of the recent attempted political coup. In Guyana, Georgetown theatre seemed to be in the very good hands of Ken Crosby and company. So I was seduced into becoming a volunteer on the grand project of building a highway through the interior of the country. The resulting play, *Down Mahdia Way*, had two rehearsals in London but no public performance.

Prior to going to the Caribbean in 1970, I made belated contact with John La Rose from Trinidad who, with his wife Sarah White, had opened the New Beacon Bookshop in Finsbury Park, bringing Caribbean books, including non-Anglophone material and work relating to Latin America and Africa, to our attention. As the bookshop was in the front room of their home, the visitor was usually encouraged – with stimulating talk and the offer of a cup of tea/coffee and, sometimes, food – to hang about.

Caribbean literature wasn't exactly unknown to me in 1970. Over the preceding decade I'd read at random John Hearne and

V. S. Naipaul as well as Jean Rhys' *Wide Sargasso Sea*. I'd struggled through much of Mittelholzer's Kaywana books and was entranced by Wilson Harris' *Palace of the Peacock*. In the late sixties Harris was a neighbour in Holland Park, and though we weren't acquainted, it was good for me to know that a substantial and visionary Caribbean presence was only a couple of hundred yards away.

My literary and academic background was something, I often felt, I was expected to apologize for. An A-level in economics was my only saving grace (other GCEs being Latin, Italian, English, History, Ancient History, etc.). Even my interests in kitchen sink drama or the Theatre of the Absurd were deemed to be English tastes. People sometimes remonstrated with you, a man from the Third World, for not aspiring to be a doctor or a lawyer or an engineer. Hence the value of my orientation course at the New Beacon Bookshop.

Once, when asked why he wrote, John La Rose said: 'Because they lie about you. They pretend to speak for you and they lie about you.' I was encouraged by this, for I thought if anyone should lie about me, I should be accorded that privilege. Though I would aim, naturally, to tell the truth.

The crash course: Earl Lovelace, Alwyn Bennett, Austin Clarke and Derek Walcott – first encountered in *London Magazine* – came close to balancing all that Anglo-Saxon and Middle English. The excitement of recognizing something of the texture of Caribbean living in the literature nevertheless occasioned a question mark in my mind. Much of the prose left me with a sense of sameness of experience which, though authentic, didn't quite capture the tone of my particular house in Montserrat. I read Lamming's *In the Castle of My Skin* and I agreed you couldn't do better than that. But was this my experience of growing up in the West Indies? It wasn't.

First of all I grew up with books in the house, lots of books that I was expected to work my way through. Alone, at night, in the drawing-room at Harris', while my grandmother had her bath next door, I picked my way through John Bunyan and *Gulliver's Travels* and something called *John Halifax*,

Gentleman – in the years before I was eleven. Gibbon's *Decline and Fall of the Roman Empire* was in the bookcase, though I didn't get round to that. And there was assorted religious material – not surprising with so many clergymen in the family. There was also a book in our bookcase called *Sinn Fein* – 'We Ourselves', as my brother translated. Montserrat was colonized in the 1620s by the Irish who proceeded to give the island that Columbus misnamed in 1493 an Irish aspect which persisted even after the British claimed it.

My grandmother was head of the household. This wasn't unusual in the West Indies: when Andrew Salkey, in a poem, talks about the 'sea split marriage' he is talking about all of us. But even when the man of the house was around, *she* was head of the household and determined all our fortunes. She had a mythical status in the village; she was known as Queen Victoria and her house was popularly dubbed 'Government house'. I remember once when the Governor wrote to her, on some matter of land registration, and signed off 'Your Humble Servant'. We children had no doubt that this man, plump and plumed and light-skinned, could be induced to bring my grandmother her water in a ewer and to fill up her nightly bathtub. A bad leg confined her to her room, but she still managed to control the house and beyond that the 'estates'. Hers was the family into which my father had married. If he proved fallible, it was her constancy that prevented us going to the dogs.

When I got back to England in 1971, among the rejected manuscripts was one from the Royal Shakespeare Company quibbling at the portrayal of the Black characters in a play I'd submitted to them the previous year. The RSC seemed to have no problem with the White characters, or with the theatrical values of the piece. After the inevitable posture of being affronted, I took a hard look at what I was doing. The father-figure was not entirely convincing. I had known that at the time of writing, and yet a sense of loyalty made me falsify his portrait. I had introduced the father as a benign ghost, sitting in the rocking chair in the drawing-room, rocking the young son – me – who was sitting on his knee. There was a story in the family that after my father left (to go off to win World War Two) I claimed the rocking chair and used to tip myself all the way forward, without falling. The family apparently looked on, confident that an invisible hand – if not the father, the grandfather behind him – kept me secure. That was the ghost figure I was trying to portray. When I was directing the Caribbean Theatre Workshop and struggling to create a convincing portrait of The Father, I wrote a little poem which seemed to sum up my difficulty at the time:

ANOTHER DAD

You're a fat old man
pleading for sympathy;

you huddle in the doorway
playing your instrument

badly – to embarrass me.
I'm your son, old man,

I'm your son
and will continue to look

the other way
till you learn to play better.

It was always difficult for me to imagine a male adult in the family, since I never had the experience of growing up in that environment. In our family the father was someone who neglected his family. But could you really call it neglect when the man went off to fight for Britain's freedom and was now a distinguished clergyman in Toronto? My brother much later supplied some of the details that would have fleshed out the portrait. Apparently when The Father returned from abroad to take over the family business after the death of my grandfather, he showed himself true to type. The business was running assorted scattered bits of land on which cotton was grown. But the man's interest lay elsewhere. He had the flower-bed at the front of the house in Harris' dug up in order to put in a new water cistern. That was the official story. In fact he was digging for buried treasure. Not finding it he had the hole filled in and the flower-bed replanted. The filled-in, replanted flower-bed settled down to being at least a foot lower than the rest of the yard, making it problematic for our subsequent cricket matches. The Father was a man who disturbed the order of the house, indeed, the aesthetic order of the house, and one was reluctant to explore fully the implications of this. Meanwhile, The Father's original continued to hide behind his clerical collar, a Very Reverend in Toronto.

Whose family is it anyway? Is it the writer's to write about or the members' to live? I accept, of course, that a writer of power and conviction must create a fictional world that is large enough to live in. I feel that the space inherited from this family is so vast that it seems dauntingly physical. When I was growing up with my grandmother, in Harris', such bedtime stories as were told weren't about Anancy or Aesop, they were about the family, the progress that her eight brothers and sisters had made in the world, the doctor in Boston, the lawyer in New York, the Justice of the Peace who went twice to England and had some sharp things to say about the state of order on the streets of London. So the role of family chronicler was one that someone had to take on. Though family members were suspicious of my increasing willingness to do it.

My brother Norman sends me newspaper cuttings and rings me with information about the house in Montserrat which he thinks I might have forgotten. And he's right. Being the youngest of four children I became fully aware of the house after it had passed its peak, so to speak. Mine is an emptyish house occupied by my grandmother and myself, along with Sarah, a young girl who worked for us and slept in. (And of course, Nellie – the Nellie of my poems who cooked and washed and, most lovingly, took care of us.) Occasionally a neighbour, a young man from the village, would sleep in the spare room when we were nervous of burglars. That was during the week. At weekends the rest of the family would come back from Plymouth – where my brothers and sister were at school – and, of course, during the holidays. Then I would be relegated to relative insignificance.

But this is 1997; I am in Sheffield. My brother rang me a few nights ago from London: did I remember the bookshelf at the bottom of the stairs, in the corner of the dining room, leading up to the drawing-room? Initially, no, but on reflection, yes. The steps leading up to the drawing-room brought something else to life. It was from those steps that I first heard my brother declaim Mark Antony's great speech, his tribute to the newly murdered Caesar, I in the dining room representing the 'marketplace', reacting like a Roman to the oration from the pulpit. He's halfway up the stairs, half turned (so he's going up) looking down on us. But that's long ago. What role is he playing now, Norman, forty years on, ringing me up from London? Not Mark Antony. Did I remember, in the corner at the foot of the stairs, inset in the wall, a ledge, a cool spot where each day Sarah placed a jar of fresh water, covered with a saucer or maybe with a white linen cloth? There were books on the shelf above the alcove. In his time, in my brother's time, someone used to read to my grandmother after her bath, at night, and one of the books they read was *Paradise Lost* taken from that shelf.

This news was intriguing because although the reading to my grandmother continued in my time, we certainly never read *Paradise Lost*. I wasn't even aware of it in the house. We read from the newspaper, careful to mispronounce words like 'rape' that we were supposed not to know; we read passages from John Bunyan and things like that, but mostly, of course, from the Bible. Every new revelation about those times makes me think I've fallen down on the job of communicating something essential about the house. It also reinforces the feeling that I'd missed out on the best of the house, that the main actors had done their thing before us and that my sister and I, the youngest, were merely understudies.

Equally intriguing are the missives from my brother, the newspaper cuttings that arrive every three weeks or so. This is general, 'improving' information, addressed to the professor (my status of academic still outweighs my profession of writer).

Among recent offerings: someone claiming to be able to teach Americans to speak a foreign language overnight; an article challenging the fundamentalists on creation; the crisis in Korea; David Edgar on 'New Writing'. The relationship between Antony and the Crowd has shifted over the years. My brother is both audience and mentor. As audience he used occasionally to come to my poetry readings in the seventies and eighties. He buys my books to give as presents. When he sees them in the shops he rings me up and talks sales. Part of his input is to hint at new things I might write.

And now I have an ungenerous thought: my brother must recognize himself in some of my fiction, for comic characteristics are taken from people I know, including family. Could it be that with these cuttings he is working to modify the image of the family I present?

WILSON HARRIS, whom I didn't really know, and Andrew Salkey apart, the few West Indian writers I'd come across in Britain seemed not to have had my experience of growing up in the region, or to be dismissive of it. So I convinced myself that they, too, were lying about me. It wasn't just my own little experience being invisibilized that made me uneasy. What of all the other families like us? West Indians and West Indianness were being defined in terms of lack or absence, or being on the periphery. That was OK, that was fine; true in a sense, though all these things *together* might not be accurate. The problem was what this was being defined against. Against England. Britain. Against an outdated idea of Englishness, preserved by us – in a way that made some wits compare us with New Zealand.

My experience of England wasn't that of plenty, despite Mr Macmillan's 'You've never had it so good' 1959 election slogan. The living standard of our family had declined in England: we didn't run a car, my mother no longer had a chauffeur, we didn't live in a house of twelve rooms with four others to our name, we didn't have servants. There was no pining for any of this – except by my mother, and she didn't go on about it – but it was an unspoken fact between us.

And in our early contacts here people didn't correspond to our notion of 'The English'. The family who rented our downstairs front room in Ladbroke Grove in the late '50s were rag-and-bone people (with children our age who eventually had to be ejected because we feared for our own hygiene). They were in line, we believe, for one of the last ten-pound-assisted passages to Australia. They were replaced by a businessman who conducted his business on the pavement. He took bets on the horses, for until Macmillan legalized the activity in time to help him win the General Election, punters had to do their trade on the pavements. But this was a definite step up because wife and daughter were respectably turned out and the daughter was also a student.

In between we had an odd experience which confirmed our growing realization that the England connection was not necessarily preferable to the West Indian one in every respect. Late one Christmas Eve my brother Norman set off to the West End – maybe to Covent Garden – where you could get the turkey at half-price or less. On his travels in the West End for the turkey he ran into a woman and child in distress. They were homeless. The husband had been violent, and they had been housed in separate places of refuge. The mother and child had left their refuge and were on the street. It was cold. It was Christmas. Norman knew that my mother would be hospitable to someone like that, particularly at Christmas. So on my mother's behalf he extended the invitation to come to the house.

My mother thought that was entirely proper, but what to do if the violent husband turned up? For Norman admitted that the wife was seeking to contact the husband. We were still debating this when the knocker went and the woman turned up, with her child. We took them in, fed them, and I, being the youngest, had to give up my bed to the mother and child and share a bed with my brother. The husband later turned up – very pleasant and contrite and hungry – and thanked us for looking after his family (my memory is faulty: it is they rather than the rag-and-bone people who were destined for Australia) before going back to his refuge. But the next morning, the mother, with her child, disappeared, having stolen my mother's purse.

I REMEMBER DEBATES in the house in Ladbroke Grove from 1956 and leading up to the 1959 General Election. We were politically unsophisticated in an English setting, having been rightish rather than leftish in a West Indian context, our largemindedness, I realized later, being nearer to paternalism than I'd like to admit. My mother liked Mr Eden's command of English. Someone on the radio complained that Mr Macmillan, who succeeded him as Tory leader and Prime Minister, was guilty of splitting his infinitives, and this was noted with interest in our house. Leaving that aside Mr Macmillan's bad teeth (clearly discernible on television) didn't appeal. These were the debates we assumed to be taking place in homes all over Britain.

We were a little bit cut off because we were in our own house. My mother had insisted on that. Not for her to be at the mercy of other people, the stony faced landladies and landlords photographed behind signs saying NO COLOUREDS, NO IRISH, NO DOGS. (We were grateful that the Irish were included, but embarrassed about the dogs.) My mother had sent on the money to my elder brothers who were barely in their twenties to buy a house. We didn't know any other West Indian families in this situation and that meant stray students and other friends from home found their way to our place, mainly at weekends, to re-experience something of the warmth of home. So it was here in late-fifties England that our re-education took place, and in 1959 some members of our family registered their first Labour vote. We quite liked Gaitskell, though we preferred Nye Bevan, because his odd-sounding Welsh voice assured us that you could be fluent in English without aping the English vowels which made us sound odd. Much later, of course, Linton Kwesi Johnson, the dub poet, came to the a similar conclusion via John Arlott, the celebrated cricket commentator whose 'Somerset burr' emphasized that there was more than one acceptable form of spoken English.

We couldn't avoid the more overt politics of the time; there was a sense, almost, of being targeted, with Oswald Mosley coming to the door. In Montserrat, in Plymouth, my mother used to sit at the upstairs window in our house on Parliament Street, looking down on the world. In our house in Ladbroke Grove she assumed the same posture. It was from here, in 1959, that she effectively attended an Oswald Mosley rally. His message was the familiar one: we West Indians were children who had been misled into coming to England. The streets of England were not paved with gold. We were unhappy to be here. It was unfair to ask us to remain in a place where we were cold and unhappy. The best thing was to send us back to a place that was warm and where we could be happy once again. That was his political programme.

We were struck by his politeness: was it right, was it a misuse of language to call it politeness? Would we rather have such ideas delivered in a reasonable tone or with the thuggishness they concealed? The crowd seemed reasonably relaxed, both assent and indignation muted. Someone in the crowd whispered that Mosley looked Jewish. Next door to us lived Geoffrey Hamm, Mosley's right-hand man in the area. He, too, was polite.

My mother, unflinching, looked down on Mosley from her window; a cousin newly in the army stood at the back of the crowd in his uniform, his arms folded. A few other West Indians stood impassive, refusing to be provoked. I joined my mother at the window. I had a sense then of a space to protect and thought, with the posture of my mother, with my army cousin in the crowd, with the calmness of the 'boys' whom we didn't know, that we wouldn't be panicked into anything, certainly not into flight. I'm talking about a view of England. It seemed short-sighted to use England as the only, or main, frame of reference when trying to bring the West Indies into focus. So I vary the frame of reference. England hasn't been my only home from home.

But why exactly do I write? It's not just self-aggrandisement. It's not even, with respect to conversations at the New Beacon Bookshop, because I want to answer back. No, it's more personal, less reactive. Back in the 1950s when I was putting press studs in belts a choice of career seemed open. One boss at the time, C.G. Spencer, liked my work and suggested – who knows how seriously? – a partnership in the belt firm in Great

Portland Street. And briefly, I did see myself as head of a leather and suede empire, belting women – average waist twenty-two inches – from Canada to Nigeria. And yet I didn't want to be consigned to the rag trade. So Spencer and I talked futures, careers. For no particular reason I said to him one day that I wanted to be a doctor. But medicine was the wrong profession for me, he said, because I didn't have the necessary love of people.

We didn't discuss this much over belts, but I couldn't entirely dislodge the feeling that I harboured a political rather than an instinctive feel for people. This contributed to my going to university to read Philosophy and English and eventually to saying rude things about Plato and Walter Pater. (Was it squeamishness rather than pain that moved me to other people's suffering? Could I get away with defining squeamishness as an aesthetic quality?) When, later, towards the end of the Nigerian Civil War, Nnamdi Azikwe, the renowned ex-president of the republic, switched from supporting the losing Biafran side, he gave a curious reason: he deplored, finally, the aesthetic spectacle of filling the world's television screens with Africans humiliating Africans, Black women humiliated, Black children brutalized, dying of kwashaqua. He appealed for an end to the war on aesthetic grounds. I felt both vindicated and appalled. I have tried ever since, through writing, to penetrate my own layers of protective skin. I write, quite simply – and it's not simple – to make myself more human.

In Other Words

Delivered in Sheffield, 26 October 1999, at the Festschrift for
E. A. Markham, arranged by Freda Volans & Tracey O'Rourke

MY FIRST IMPULSE, of course, is to welcome so many consenting family and friends and colleagues – to the party – to welcome you to this event. I feared, perhaps, that no one would turn up. I'm not, after all, in a position of, say, the popular Syrian poet Mustapha Thass, who gets whole regiments of people to turn up at his soirées in downtown Damascus. Of course Mustapha Thass happens to be Minister of Defence in the Syrian government, and is able to assist his readers with their transport. But then, perhaps it isn't my role anyway, to welcome you. That might be a bit presumptuous because I'm not, in a real sense, the host. So etiquette demands that I thank you, my friends, for inviting me to your very special party. At this point, I think, I'm expected to say that I'm in no way worthy of this honour. So we're agreed on that. Welcome anyway. Welcome.

Relieved thanks to Jeremy Poynting and Hannah Bannerman for doing such a superb job on the *festschrift* publication, and special thanks to Elaine Bull for a proofreading effort without which we would all have been embarrassed.

But y'know, some sort of apology *is* in order for the *name*, if nothing else, of the event: what is a *festschrift*? We are not German, though some of us, happily, are. Again, let me thank Ann Volans – Freda, Fred – and Tracey O'Rourke for editing the text: what I owe you can't be repaid in one lifetime, so we're talking afterlife now, ghost-time, jumbie-time. So let me assure you, Fred and Tracey, that my jumbie (who will haunt only literary enemies) will spare you both a visit. For a West Indian that is the ultimate act of self-denial. Dear friends . . .

When I knew we were doing a *festschrift* – you're supposed not to know these things, but you have to be sounded out – in case you're late back from the launderette that day. Or at least to establish that you'll be in the country – it intrigued me to know how I might weigh the honour, how I might best describe the event. So, naturally, I turned to the dictionary. *The Oxford English* – not keeping up with the modernizing tendency of our times – didn't feel able to include the word. Nothing, either, in the majestic one-volume *Webster Comprehensive International Dictionary of the English Language*. Even the *Oxford Universal* evidently thought the term not universal enough for English consumption.

But when you're desperate (and colleagues who work at Hallam know all about desperation) you persist. *The Penguin Dictionary of Literary Terms* has a definition rather too heavy for comfort. Among other things it says: 'The term denotes a symposium – symposium – compiled in honour of a distinguished scholar or writer.' Well, even my best friends . . . However . . . A man called F. C. Scott, in his 1965 book *Current Literary Terms*, says that the *festschrift* is written or published on the subject's retirement or birthday. So there we are: between a Rock and a Hard Place. But to return to *festschrift*.

What might let us off the, shall we say, lexical hook is that the compilers of the Chambers *Twentieth Century Dictionary* have, indeed, seen fit, not just to include the term, but to *anglicize* it: it's no longer in italics. (The German root is acknowledged. But Festschrift is described simply as 'a festival publication, commonly a collection of learned papers' – and here I shift the embarrassment from me to you, my friends – 'learned papers *or the like*, presented by their authors and published in honour of *some* person.' Now, the weight of that is more bearable; easier to live with. So, again, friends, family, Romans (The Romans aren't here yet. The History of Britain is being unwritten.) Colleagues. Thank you.

(You will recall, those of you who read David Lodge, the fairly pivotal role in driving the plot that the *festschrift* assumes in his campus novel *Changing Places*.)

Now, let me congratulate you for being able to find the university. Not everyone has been so fortunate. Some friends phoned earlier, a dear couple with a youngish child, seeking directions. And I did the usual things, trying to steer them through Sheffield's one-way system; to the top of the road, to

Park Lane, and a big sign that says UNIVERSITY. There you enter University space. A place of calm and harmony pulsing with the true sensuality of higher learning. The parents were prepared to go along with this, but the child, who has a reputation for being precocious, wanted to know whether she could trust the sign. Could we trust a sign on a building saying University to be accurate? Well – they're our future intake. I readily conceded that we sometimes made mistakes, and no doubt the workmen and women, who put up the signs occasionally made mistakes. But I was a bit slow on the uptake; this was an unusual child: What, she asked, if the workmen and women hadn't made a mistake. But were really clever and did it as a practical joke! Sometimes, you know, life can be very long. But when you're 60, and they tell you you'd better start getting used to tripping, not on interesting substances, but on the broken paving-stones of Life, you learn to be patient.

So I said to the child: I sighed and told her, patiently as I could, that up here in the North, we were either too grown-up or ground down to indulge in practical jokes. This was a solid, northern town, this was a hard-won new university and that – since the child was being playful – that in fictional terms the workmen and women in putting up the sign were more likely to conform to the laws of narrative rather than *magical* realism, than in sending clever messages through symbols. So I went on to describe bits of the university she might recognize. The building round the corner, for instance, where the women who had recently won the Nobel Prize for soil chemistry were taking time off for their weekly Tai Chi session prior to writing up the new breakthrough that would, y'know, help to do all the right things for the badlands of the Southern Sahara. You know, and so on: General tour of the campus. Past the Library, where there was still a book to be found tucked away somewhere among the computers and videos for Film Studies, that sort of thing. The lawns, the hedges, untended today because the workmen and women being Hallam workmen and women would be at home catching up on their reading, and having quality time to themselves to ponder, say, the condition of Austria. My description of the University in these terms was clearly wide of the mark, because my friends haven't yet turned up. Sorry. So thank you, specially, for your sense of direction.

You would expect me to say something about the business of being a writer, and to do it at great length. (It says here, pause for laughter.) But seriously, I know some of you need to get back to London to resume work on the Ken Livingstone for Mayor campaign. We'll be joining you later. OK, I know a couple of people here need to get back to attend John Birt's BBC farewell bash at Hampton Court tomorrow night. But we won't let on. So, to the business of writing:

FROM THE JUMBLE of obsessions that provokes the work to the feedback which keeps you puzzled and in need of psychiatric help: what to drag out? I've just published a campus novel, a university novel set here at Hallam and elsewhere. It's had an interesting reception. Now that I'm seen as the man who writes campus novels I find that people I run into at work, in this building, seem actively to be auditioning for roles in the next novel. Small-talk at lunch, in the corridors, in the kitchen is now peppered with unexpected witticisms, aphorisms; with extended similes often to do with the environment – comparing the brewing of herbal tea to the educative process, sort of thing. And much quoting dead authors. It's a bit of a shock first thing in the morning to run into Dave. (I call everyone at work Dave, not that they look alike particularly. But it's a good new university name. And there are worse things in life than being called Dave. Though some of the women think I might do better. So what's new.)

'Morning Dave', you say, as you enter the kitchen. And Dave looks up and says:

'Show me the man who asks an over-abundant share

Of life, in love with more, and ill-content with less.'

And . . . Yeah. Nice one. Pre-campus novel Dave would merely have said something like:

'What, so what have I done, now?'

I'm not picking on an individual, of course. You go past others in the foyer, and hear one saying to another:

'O, Dave, I managed to get you that room for your "Minority with Unrepresentative Views" seminar.' (We do have to recruit.)

And Dave says: 'Thank you, gentle Hopkins', slipping softly into Shakespearean mode. Enough of Dave.

I suppose the footnote is that colleagues who see bits of themselves portrayed in the campus novel, very properly wish to contest their representation in the narrative. No problem with that. The puzzle is that they tend sometimes, when wearing their academic hat, to indulge students with the heresy of the death of the author. Look around this room, I say to you, and recant.

But why am I avoiding talking about writing? What value to place on this activity which some regard as a form of self-indulgence – injurious to your health? Well, they're right there. The costs are fairly clear to me: I have a pain in my arm (My arm, now prisoner to the palsy); the effect of *cervical spondychosis*, in itself the effect of 40 years of manual typing. Now, dear reader, I have a computer; and on that computer I manage to lose quite a few things, including the stray comments I had planned to make today. So, these are, if you like, substitute words. But as one has a sense, always, of ending up using the wrong words, censorship by computer is not terminal. Indeed, in the *festschrift* there is a poem of mine about using the wrong words, translated into both German and Italian. My German and Italian translators, Silke Kasuch and Maria Antoanetta Saracino and Bruno Gallo are tactful and humane people. Remember translators are your closest readers: they are the ones who find you out. (I'm planning a book, a thriller where the crazed writer goes around murdering all his potential translators, in advance of writing the book. But you are safe, the writer is inefficient; and the book is a comedy.)

But I'm relieved translators draw different inferences from me about my using the wrong words in the first place, and then expecting them to labour over the translation of those words. When, over the last three decades or so, in gender politics, in First-World/Third-World discourse – to name but two battlefields – ownership of the vocabulary has been a key issue, then to persist in using the wrong words isn't a very clever literary stratagem. I have sometimes been ambivalent about my voice reproduced in English. And having listened to my words in German and in Italian, I find the unease increased three-fold.

I know I'm being precious. Every artist of ambition experiences the futility of finding an idiom to match and communicate something of the mystery of human consciousness. (Existence isn't a mystery, particularly; consciousness is.) You're not alone in being humbled in having got it wrong. In good moments you put it down to the condition of the art, or to the cycle – does this sound familiar? – at which you enter the evolution of the language, of the *genre*. (You might even fantasize about – why not? – Leonardo who towards the end of his life expressed two regrets: *one*, that he had never completed sculpting his great Milanese horse and *two*, that he never learnt to fly. And he might not have been talking aeroplanes. Or balloons. That's one end of the scale. At the other more familiar end you plug in to your old neuroses of, oh, of being short-changed in the market of talent, and needing to accept with grace and resignation – Hello Grace: old joke – you accept with grace and resignation what cannot be accepted with grace and resignation. Yes, to lament the gap between ambition and achievement will keep us, not young, dear reader, but juvenile to the end. Even now I can hear myself using the wrong words. In other words . . .)

Much is made in the *festschrift* of my various personae. I have acknowledged to being Markham, Paul St. Vincent. And Sally Goodman (but not yet to being Silas Tomkyn Comberbache). And you know, this is a lot less problematic than forever being confused with the man who used to read the News at Ten on ITV, or the Ghanaian Secretary-General on the whatever floor it is at the top of the UN building in New York. Masks or selves, they ask. Why so showy about adopting all these selves when other writers negotiate the same variation of voice and range of sensibility, but more discreetly?

Maybe I've suffered too many thefts of *self* over the years to be secure in having just one. I remember being invited to a conference in Stockholm sometime in the eighties, a British Council tour, a group of us from Black Arts in Britain. I couldn't make the trip. But someone who could apparently gave my speech, more or less word-perfect, unattributed. He did it well; I was no longer needed; I would have to seek new ways to impersonate myself. This, you know, was not unlike the position of Borges, poet and fabulist, from Argentina, whose impulse towards more and more innovation in his prose was driven by the need to leave his imitators behind. (Not that I'm making literary comparisons between myself and Borges.) So maybe something more down-to-earth will come to the rescue. Tanzania.

An incident at the Tanzanian High Commission in London in the mid-1970s comes to mind. But, of course, I can't talk now about Tanzania without remembering our Mwalimu, Nyerere. Julius Nyerere, who was buried earlier this week. Nyerere; a scholar-translator of Shakespeare – wise and graceful and full of humour – and with the necessary cunning to admit his faults; and even those who opposed him agreed that neither the reality of power nor the prospect of wealth made him turn into something strange – whose rhythm of life made sense. And I'd like to take this opportunity to read a little poem in remembrance. It's translated from the Korean; and it's called 'A Name'.

> My name is nothing special:
> it simply means the good 'gargler'.
> In the morning I wash in the stream,
> fill my mouth with water,
> spew it high in the sky,
> and greet the rising sun
> with a flash of laughing teeth.
> People liked this,
> so they called me the gargler.
> In Chinese it is written *myong-rim-o-su*,
> the gargler from the house of Myongnim.
> I have no other exceptional skill
> – once, though, I was Prime Minister.

Now, none of this alters the fact that I was robbed at the Tanzanian High Commission in London. Of little bits of paper. Degree and other certificates – including one recently acquired from a building *Cooperative* in the South of France, where, for two years I was a member helping to design, restore and build houses. Now, I would not then (or ever) have called myself a master *maçon*, but that's what my leaving certificate said. I was mortified to have had it stolen. More, I was terrified that it would fall into the wrong hands – some adventurous property developer putting up skyscrapers in Dar-es-Salaam, in my name. Wouldn't you, too, have gone into hiding?

But, nearer home, I *am* sensitive to what is hinted at in my hiding behind personae, to the psychological and political inferences drawn: that one comes from the edge of Empire (first of the United Kingdom, now of the United States); that coming from the edge of Empire one draws – like Kamau Brathwaite of Barbados, like Derek Walcott of St. Lucia – the sustenance that ah, Yeats didn't intend from his apocalyptic line: 'Things fall apart/the centre cannot hold.' For what we tell ourselves is that those of us who inherit the language inherit important bits of the kingdom. And we support Walcott's assertion that 'culture is where the language is'. And yet, you can't escape that soft and persistent midnight voice which nudges you away from sleep: *you are being used*, it says. *They are clever. Their voice is widely discredited. You are the new agent, employed to make it palatable to those who might be squeamish.* And you wake and think. Yes. If only one self is being taken in, that's fine. I have others. Maybe that's why I pretend to be other people. In any case, one self is too risky; you need cover.

As you know I teach Creative Writing at this institution. And we're so keen to validate the process of writing (rather than simply the *result*) that we like to deny that there's any such thing as a false start. If it doesn't work your perception that it doesn't work is part of the learning process. Another pair of eyes will see a way out of that particular trap. Or a period of reflection will do it. Or even something less strenuous – Nixon's famous 'benign neglect', his policy towards African-Americans – might do it. When you come back to it, having lived other bits of your life, the difficulty encountered seems solvable, the space which you found so cramped has been miraculously enlarged, the space that was too narrow for manoeuvre. The broken-down lorry – to change the metaphor – Trevor Bailey, the cricket commentator, says it's OK to mix your metaphors – the broken-down lorry which caused the jam has been towed away without anyone being aware of it. The traffic suddenly surges forward, and your writing cul-de-sac has turned into a thoroughfare. (Your problem now is knowing how to drive.) So there's no such thing as a false start in writing. Writing, in that sense, is infinitely more forgiving than life – until writing helps you to deal with that conviction.

These thoughts about false starts are provoked by my having had to pack up bits of my apprentice work for a university purchasing my archives. When someone asks about the value of what you write you tend not to include what you reject. You're not even in the position of the celebrity whose memorabilia goes to auction. This week, I believe, in New York Christie's are holding an auction of Marilyn Monroe's dresses and silk pyjamas, cheese-graters, colanders, etc. If that is subject to healthy scepticism, how much more vulnerable your misspellings, and how stable your evidence that there's no such thing as a false start.

Looking at the literary baggage destined for the archives, I can't help registering something like dismay. For things were broken off with the expectation that one would return to them: one assumed, then, a life somewhat longer than one's life. Getting rid of your fragments now is making a statement about mortality. Is this the best you could do for your constituency – family, friends, translators – who have supported you? The very least you can do is to acknowledge that there has been wastage. Of course that midnight voice tells you that it's worse than that. That there is something not quite moral here. That all those unrealized scenes and undeveloped Characters; deformities that have enough life to be monstrous – that's all you need to be human – but not enough art to respect what is human, including oneself – makes you question whether the later work provides enough of a corrective. It's time for panic; for frenzy. But fortunately, there are wise heads around, like Ken Parker's here – still, mysteriously, on his body – who caution you to 'hasten slow'.

But I do have fantasies of Pushkin. I think of the occasion of Pushkin's birthday each year. The non-literary people of St. Petersburg turning out to celebrate their great poet. Bakers and Butchers and shopkeepers, dressed as Pushkin characters, riding through the streets in livery in carriages. Or on foot, turning the 26th of May into a literary street festival. In my nightmares I contrast this with someone who knows me, let loose on my literary archives; a literary enemy, or an academic, mean and malignant, foraging among my false starts and coming up with a pantomime. There is a car in one early sketch. It's not a car, it's an idea for car; it doesn't even have a make, never mind an engine and wheels. Again, in this one, another sketch, the snatch of dialogue can come out of any mouth, for there is no individual life informing it. So the riot in the stage directions doesn't happen as the speakers are not peopled or grounded enough to have grievances. (Death scenes were abandoned early on, for the external world did this sort of thing so much better.) In another fragment there is a kitchen scene. This is from a play, late 1950s, I should imagine. Someone (or rather someone's name) is at the sink. The tap is turned on.

The scene is Ladbroke Grove. That was over 40 years ago. And the tap has not been turned off. I feel guilty about Ladbroke Grove. Surely by now it must be flooded. (If this were written up at the right time – late 1950s – it would have fitted the style of the time, the *Theatre of the Absurd*. But time has passed, as they say, and we must put away childish things, with our Ionesco.) Now, having made so much water in Ladbroke Grove, I feel guilty about the waste of the world's resources. If I do not turn off that tap some alien government might come to power and threaten to privatize our water. I must finish the scene and save us from that catastrophe.

So I make the connections – the person in the call-box in Ladbroke Grove in 1956, who couldn't get through, can now get through to the person at the other end. But that person now brings 40 years of having lived a parallel life, and the consequences have to be faced. So is the vision of fiction textured by the life of the writer.

I MUST MENTION my mother. She misses out in my writing to my grandmother. The grandmother is fictionally alive and well and, what, 130-odd years old; she's my passport to immortality; I don't have problems with that. (I've lived in New Guinea and in England; Ancestor-worship seems just fine.)

The family thing is important to negotiate. Michael Holroyd, in his new family memoir *Basil Street Blues*, quotes Philip Roth as saying that once a writer is born into a family, that family is finished. And in a sense this is true: in one sense you're asking your family to do a strip-tease in front of strangers. Now, here is my mother in this fragment. She is in the supermarket. She is at the dairy counter contemplating the eggs. Maybe 'contemplation' is too certain a description for what she is doing. She's not actively contrasting the free-range product with the others: that would be a sign of the author pressuring the subject, nudging her into analogy of her own condition, freer in the Caribbean, more cramped in England. (And that perception might be untrue.) She mustn't be conventionalized in this way. So there she is, maybe contemplating the eggs. (There is a note in the margin where I seem to suggest she might be called Socrates, but that doesn't make sense now because she didn't really play football.)

She is muttering to herself. Passing customers take note. Not all of them unsympathetic, though someone wanting to get at the eggs is wary. The scene ends here. What didn't find form is her weighing up the large box of eggs against the extra large box of eggs. Not the price, she doesn't notice that. Just the fact that things can now be arranged in this way, and her uncertainty of whether others in her condition (proud but determined not to be showy) would go for the large or the extra large eggs. And as this is England and there's no one to ask, she stands there muttering and her story, her poem, her play doesn't get written, her life not filled out. It still seems important to be loyal to your subject. Aristotle says somewhere, rightly I think, that virtue is cultivated by the practise of virtuous acts. I liken this writer's inner loyalty to his subject as one, perhaps feeble, attempt at virtue.

(As late as 1972 I published a poem called 'The Optimist'. And of course one is still optimistic: there's no compelling reason, really, why one is alive and in reasonably good health and not battling for survival in some civil war somewhere. One had a privileged childhood in the Caribbean, and in the London of the '50s. Supportive family. Indulgent friends. And colleagues generous to a fault of one's eccentricities. Now my optimism, I'm afraid, is something more self-willed, not unlike that of the good Lady Antonia Fraser, who came on the television recently to fantasize about winning the National Lottery. She wanted to win, I quote, 'lots and lots of money. So I could give it all to the Health Service'.)

Before I end – I will, perhaps, read a poem about Montserrat later, that's why I've made no mention of Montserrat – let me just return for a minute to this business of masks, disguises, personae. It is a truism that those of us who come from small islands – Cuba, Haiti, Jamaica, St. Lucia, etc. – tend, perhaps in compensation, to write epics. It is clear that when the living space is very small the need to break out is irresistible. One's condition is therefore that of a refugee. Either part of you is elsewhere. Or part of you is preparing to move on. Having moved on, you lose the security of being part of the norm. You are in a minority. Some minorities can, within a generation or less merge themselves with the majority. That makes sense. It is a sign of fantastic recklessness to be always in a society where you are always going to be in the minority. At worst minorities are persecuted or killed. At best minorities are noticed when they have no wish to be noticed, to draw unacceptable attention to themselves. A young black man in an MG in Paddington or Stoke Newington will provoke a mating call from a police car. An Asian in the Lords will get death threats. This is as good as it gets. If these concerns don't overwhelm my work, I expect at least a few readers to note the author's restraint in these matters. This comes from a stubborn, wilful, frayed, and historically incorrect decision to remain optimistic. Meanwhile – for I'm living far from home – I will continue working on my disguises. (In the completed sketch in the supermarket, in the diary, my mother might well be thinking: how it is that the Hungarians who came over with us in 1956, waves of others since then, the Albanians today will soon be indistinguishable from the majority while her grandchildren and great-grandchildren will remain, forever, ethnic. Eggs. She's not thinking about eggs.)

And finally, I return to the business of the *festschrift*, having started with it – my pretension to give these few comments some semblance of shape. Though I am not a scholar, I work in a scholarly environment. In the corridor the other day, just outside, I ran across some colleagues making some rather erudite jokes about Linguistics. The original joke had something to do with 'morphemes', and much hilarity resulted. Now, a 'morpheme' – I am a layman, I look these things up. Or I ask my colleagues to explain – a morpheme is a unit of linguistic form, a word, a meaningful part of a word. I shared the joke that day and have since had time to reflect. That's why I am now grateful that my scholarly friends and others have had the generosity to put together not *A Morpheme* for Sally Goodman. Or for Paul St. Vincent. Or for Silas Tomkyn Comberbache . . . Not that, but a *festschrift* for E. A. Markham. Thank you. Thank you very much.

26 *October* 1999

Notes

7   *Zog*: Ahmed Bey Zogu (1895–1961), a highland, tribal chieftain, proclaimed himself King of Albania, in 1928.

31   *de Lawrence*: purveyor, from America, of mail-order esoteric knowledge, often practised as a supplement to 'church' religion. Influenced some of the founders of Rastafarianism.

34   *Like the son of a tailor*: Columbus was actually the son of a wool-comber.

34   *Intuitives*: a less pejorative title than 'primitives'. Used of a group of Jamaican painters who came to prominence in the 1970s. Prominent figures in the 'movement' include Sidney McLaren, Sam Brown, Feea Daughter of Zion and pre-eminently Everald Brown, Malleca Reynolds, Kapo and John Dunkley.

36   *mysteriously, in Luton*: after the Montserrat volcano in 1995 some families were temporarily resettled in Britain, some who missed out on Birmingham and Manchester ended up in Luton.

40   *festschrift*: see pp. 105 ff.

45   *The island, whose name you never knew*: the name of the island which Columbus seemed not to know was Allouagana, the Carib name for Montserrat.

61   pre-*Tiger*, pre-*Fearless*: in 1966 and 1968 HMS *Tiger* and HMS *Fearless* were the scenes of Harold Wilson's meetings with Rhodesian leader Ian Smith who, in 1965, had declared unilateral independence for the colony.

64   *Liz to his Richard*: Elizabeth Taylor and Richard Burton sailed down the Danube in some style to celebrate one of their marriages.

64   *her Pope's right boot*: Pope Martin. In the entrance to the church in Tody near Arezzo, the 12th-century Pope Martin sits on his throne. The rust-coloured sculpture has one startling feature – the Pope's extended boot is polished golden by the hands of visitors to the church.

87   *Anna Livia Plurabelle*: the lady in *Finnegan's Wake*.

91   *an environment of self-improvement*: the academic experience of my father must have been a factor. As a mature student after

World War II, in which he fought, he acquired degrees at McGill and elsewhere in North America (B.D., M.Th., D.D.) and ended up as a Very Reverend in Toronto.

94   *in the drawing room at Harris'*: Harris' (pronounced Harrises) is a village in the East of Montserrat, which was the principal family home.

110   *Silas Tomkyn Comberbache* was the name the young Coleridge chose, when he abandoned Cambridge briefly in 1793 to enlist as a trooper in the Light Dragoons.

111   The poem is from *Poems of a Wanderer* by Midang So Chong-Ju, translated by Kevin O'Rourke (Dedalus Press, 1995).

New and Recent Poetry from Anvil

Anvil New Poets 3
edited by Roddy Lumsden & Hamish Ironside

Gavin Bantock
Just Think of It

Oliver Bernard
Verse &c.

Nina Bogin
The Winter Orchards

Michael Hamburger
Intersections

James Harpur
Oracle Bones

Anthony Howell
Selected Poems

Marius Kociejowski
Music's Bride

Peter Levi
Viriditas

Gabriel Levin
Ostraca

Thomas McCarthy
Mr Dineen's Careful Parade

Dennis O'Driscoll
Weather Permitting

Greta Stoddart
At Home in the Dark

Daniel Weissbort
What Was All the Fuss About?